Olivier de Vleeschouwer

ROSES
MADE EASY

photographs by
Joëlle Caroline Mayer & Gilles Le Scanff

HACHETTE
Illustrated

ROSES

MADE EASY

Publisher: Élisabeth Darets
Artistic and editorial directors: Emmanuel Le Vallois, Rose-Marie Di Domenico
and Sophie Coupard
Production: Laurence Ledru
Colour separations: Reproscan

© Hachette 2004 (Marabout)
This edition © 2005 Hachette Illustrated UK, Octopus Publishing Group Ltd.,
2-4 Heron Quays, London E14 4JP
English translation by JMS Books LLP
(email: moseleystrachan@blueyonder.co.uk)
Translation © Octopus Publishing Group Ltd.

A CIP catalogue for this book is available from the British Library

ISBN-13: 978-1-84430-132-4

ISBN-10: 1-84430-132-X

Printed in Singapore by Tien Wah Press

Foreword

WIDELY HELD TO BE THE FLOWER AMONG FLOWERS, THE ROSE OCCUPIES a special place in every gardener's heart. It seems that many a passion for gardening has stemmed from a chance encounter with a rose. Once etched in the memory, the merest hint of its fragrance in the air instantly transports us back to that very first meeting. For Citizen Kane, it was his 'Rosebud', but for many others it was simply stumbling across a 'Crimson Glory' or 'Cardinal de Richelieu', their majestic, dark red flowers and heady perfumes ensnaring the unwary victim for life. Once enslaved, we are powerless to resist, 'Now that you have met me, you will never forget me!' What are the thorns of these seemingly innocent creatures for, if not to get us completely hooked? Whether gazing at the sweetly framed face of a 'Comte de Chambord' or the glorious bloom of a 'Nevada', we find ourselves drawn to the beauty of the rose everywhere, in nurseries, flower shows, rose gardens... in our tireless quest for sensual experience. When you are a rose-lover, you can find a thousand ways to heap praise on them – even when none is strictly due. How many other flowers are there where a lack of fragrance becomes a fragrance in its own right? After all, roses with no perfume of their own are simply said to smell of pure, fresh air.

However much you love roses, faced with the thousands of varieties available, with new ones being created each year, just how do you make your choice? With no attempt at disguising a certain partiality, this book presents you with a set of choices using practical criteria: what sort of Climbers do you want?... pink roses or red ones?... which varieties will thrive on your balcony?... which roses never get sick?... The same down-to-earth approach is taken with the practical information on care and cultivation. There's no reason to over-complicate matters – to succeed with roses, all you really need is a few practical tips and a great deal of love.

Wander through these pages as if meandering along a path in a garden. Lean over, cup a flower in your hand and breathe in its fragrance. Move on, and then retrace your steps. Close your eyes and imagine how you would like your garden to look. Roses begin by inhabiting our dreams. The act of planting them is simply proof that they really exist.

Opposite: *Rosa* 'American Pillar' and *Campanula persicifolia*.
Pages 4 and 5: *Rosa glauca, Berberis thunbergii* 'Rose Glow' and *Salix purpurea* 'Nana'.

A brief history

No species of rose are found naturally in the Southern hemisphere, but in the Northern hemisphere, roses can grow in the wild – such as the pretty dog rose with its single, five-petalled flowers that scrambles through hedgerows in early summer. These are the true ancestors of the three thousand or so varieties of rose that we grow today in our gardens. Old Roses stem from these wild roses. Flowering just once each year, their perfume is frequently intensely fragrant and their reputation for hardiness is well deserved.

The oldest group of roses, *Rosa gallica*, was already widespread by the time of the ancient Greeks and the Romans. These, together with the *Albas* (whose colours vary from pure white to a flesh-pink), were the two main types of rose grown in Europe up to the 13th century.

Damask Roses (*Damascena*), which are paler in colour than the *Gallicas*, were brought to Europe at the time of the Crusades. One of the Crusaders, Thibaut IV of Champagne, took back to France a *Rosa gallica* that became known as the Provins Rose as it was grown widely for its petals around the town of Provins. In England it was adopted by the House of Lancaster as their official emblem and was also known as the Apothecary's Rose (*Rosa Gallica officinalis*) owing to its use in perfumed waters and medicinal peparations.

As early as the sixteenth century, a group of Dutch botanists created a hybrid from *Albas* and Damask Roses. Known as the *Centifolia* or 'hundred-leaved rose' (at that time, 'leaves' meant 'petals'), this full-bloomed rose (also known as the Cabbage Rose) quickly became prominent in the decorative arts and was seen everywhere, even on pottery and ceramics. Moss Roses are very similar to *Centifolias,* apart from the characteristic moss-like surface of their sepals and flower stem.

The introduction of the China Rose and Slater's Crimson China, brought back to Europe by a captain in the British East India Company at the end of the 18th century, started a real revolution in the world of roses. It was the cross-breeding of these two roses with Old Roses that gave us the modern varieties we have today. Without these two roses, the modern repeat flowering varieties that bloom several times in the course of one season would just not exist.

Another variety of rose from China, Tea Roses (*Rosa odorata*), were introduced into Europe at the beginning of the 19th century. Their highly fragrant flowers quickly became a favourite with many people.

Throughout the 19th century, the activities of the rose growers bordered on the frenetic and many new groups were created, including many of the most famous, such as Bourbon, Noisette, Tea-Noisette and Portland.

Crossing Bourbon Roses with *Gallicas, Centifolias,* Damasks and Tea Roses produced a strain of repeat flowering hybrids upon which many hopes were pinned. Unfortunately, these roses quickly proved to be poor repeaters, with little resistance to disease.

However, the rose growers' determination finally paid off with the successful marriage of a repeat flowering hybrid and a Tea Rose, and the Hybrid Tea, the Modern Rose *par excellence*, was born. With 'La France', created in 1867, Guillot launched a new generation of roses that were called Hybrid Teas or large-flowered roses. These roses are both sturdy and elegant, and best of all, they flower continuously.

In the 20th century, the Hybrid Teas continued to be the focus of attention for rose-growers, who also created the *Polyanthas* and the *Floribundas*, as well as the first Prostrate, or Ground-cover roses that grow along the ground horizontally.

As if this huge choice of varieties were not enough, horticulturalists still continue to battle to produce new varieties by combining the best characteristics from existing strains in an effort to produce Modern Roses that will repeat flower and remain disease-free, yet also be endowed with the beauty and the lasting charm of some of the Old Roses.

The history of hybridisation may seem a little complex, but don't worry, your knowledge of the intricacies of the rose family tree will not affect your ability to grow them successfully!

Opposite: *Rosa* **'New Dawn'**
and *Clematis florida* **'Sieboldii'.**

Rose shapes and planting positions

You know you'd like to grow some roses in your garden – but which ones should you choose? A visit to some established gardens or specialist rose-nurseries will soon help you become familiar with the different varieties available and their varying shapes, types of flower, fragrance and habit. Armed with this knowledge, you'll find it much easier to make an informed choice, taking into account both your preferences, and the size of your garden or patio.

Bush Roses (Floribunda and Hybrid Tea)

The Bush Rose is what we think of as the classic rose; it usually reaches a height of between 50cm (20in) and 120cm (4ft). There are two types: the large-flowered or Hybrid Tea Rose, usually with a single bloom on each stem, and the cluster-flowering rose with trusses of several blooms on each stem (Polyantha and Floribunda).

The large-flowered Hybrid Tea varieties produce the most fragrant roses and the best roses for cutting, although they generally bloom less frequently than the Floribunda, while the Polyantha and Floribunda make a good show when used in large beds and in mixed borders.

Shrub Roses

Shrub Roses are hard to categorise as there are so many different forms, but they are all vigorous growers, bushy in habit and with a range of different flower shapes (single or double), and include many beautiful Old-fashioned Roses. Some are compact in habit, growing only to about 90cm (3ft) while others can grow up to 1.5–2m (5ft–6ft 6in) in both height and breadth, depending on the variety. The repeat flowering types can flower from mid-May to October. Shrub Roses look good either grown singly or in groups of three; they can be planted in a lawn or in a border where they will blend in with other shrubs and perennials. Their generous, ample shape lends a special charm to their appearance.

Climbing and Rambling Roses

Both types of rose can be made to climb, but there are several differences between the two. Climbers have stiff, straight stems and are best grown against rigid structures such as walls or trellis. Ramblers are more vigorous with more pliable stems and a naturally meandering habit – they can climb over many different kinds of support, from an old tree to an unsightly building that you may want to hide. Climbers have larger flowers and are often repeat flowering, the flowers growing on new growth produced earlier in the year, while Ramblers generally flower with clusters of small blooms just once on the previous year's growth. Both Climbers and Ramblers need to be attached to their support with ties. Some varieties reach a height of 3–5m (9–15ft), while Ramblers can grow 6–15m (18–45ft) high.

Ground-cover (Prostrate Roses)

The low-growing, spreading habit of these roses makes them ideal ground-cover plants, suitable for use on banks, in paved areas or at the front of a border. If allowed to grow unchecked, they will generally spread up to 3m (9ft) in width and up to about 30.5cm (12ins) in height, although some can reach nearly a metre (40ins), or even more. Some Ground-cover Roses flower once, while others are repeat flowering from summer to autumn.

Miniature Roses

Due to their small size, growing to about 50cm (20in) in height, these roses inevitably look out of place in any but the smallest of gardens, but they are ideal for tubs and make very decorative window-boxes. They make up for their lack of fragrance with profuse flowering, which occurs from summer to the first frosts.

Standard Roses

Standard Roses are normal Bush Roses grafted on to a straight stem. On a half-standard the graft is generally made at a height of about 60cm (24in) and on a full standard at about 110cm (3ft 6in). Weeping Standards are obtained by grafting a climbing variety onto a stem at about 180cm (6ft). Due to the formal and 'architectural' nature of their shape, Standard Roses can look out of place in certain positions, such as set in a lawn, although this position suits a Weeping Standard well. However, they add an elegant finishing touch if their striking shape is used to good effect, such as flanking a door or forming the focal point in a bed or border.

Ten growing tips

1   Which rose where?

2   Buy healthy plants

3   Plant at the right time

4   Space plants correctly

5   Tend the soil

6   Tend grafting points

7   Remember to feed and water

8   Treat any diseases

9   Don't forget to dead-head

10 Pruning is not as hard as you think!

Useful information

Useful tools

A good gardener always uses good tools. It pays to go for good quality, even if it costs a little more; choose tools with strong handles that are firmly secured and buy a pair of by-pass secateurs whose scissor-like action will ensure a clean cut. Tools have a much longer life if they are properly looked after, so, after every use, get into the habit of giving them a wipe with an old cloth to remove any traces of damp soil from the metal and wooden parts. The occasional drop of oil rubbed over the metal will stop any rust taking hold. Blades should be sharpened regularly.

Spade and fork
Both a spade and a fork are indispensable. A spade is used for turning the soil over and for digging planting holes, and also provides a good way of getting a tidy edge to a lawn. Where the soil is stony or more compacted, using a fork will help loosen it first.

Onion hoe *(top left)*
Also called a hand or rock garden hoe, this is useful for weeding between plants that are positioned closely together, minimising damage to the plants themselves.

Combined hoe and fork *(not shown)*
Two tools in one, the combination hoe is invaluable for weeding. Weeds can be cut and removed with the blade of the hoe, while the prongs help break up the soil.

Daisy grubber *(not shown)*
This is extremely useful for digging out long-rooted weeds such as dandelions.

Hand cultivator *(left, second from top)*
Various types are available. Their main use is for aerating the soil between plants, without damaging them at the base.

Secateurs *(top right)*
No rose-lover should ever be without a pair of secateurs in his or her pocket – it's the one tool that is really essential. Used for pruning and for general tidying up, choose a pair of by-pass secateurs that can cut a thickness of up to 1cm ($\frac{1}{2}$in). There are many types available, so make sure you choose a pair that you find comfortable to use.

Loppers *(not shown)*
For branches 1–2.5cm ($\frac{1}{2}$–1in) in diameter, use loppers (or long-handled pruners) rather than secateurs. Their long handles allow you to avoid stretching and to work where access is difficult. Before buying , make sure the loppers feel right for you – bear in mind that you may have to hold them at arm's length, which will be tiring if they are heavy.

Pruning saw *(not shown)*
If you need to cut old wood which is hard and very dense, or stems over 2cm ($\frac{3}{4}$in) in diameter, a pruning saw could prove useful. Its curved shape will help you work in a confined space or where access is awkward.

Thick gloves
Some varieties of rose have extremely sharp thorns, so make sure that your gloves are thick enough to give your hands proper protection, while allowing your fingers some movement and flexibility.

Watering-can and hosepipe
It goes without saying that these are indispensable. To keep your roses in top condition, water them at the base and avoid splashing the leaves.

Insect spray
Even if you have sworn to be completely 'green', let the ladybirds do their job and never use chemicals, you may find you have to resort to an insect spray eventually. Only spray when there is no wind.

Ties
If you want your roses to climb over a wall or a pergola, they will need to be secured to their support. Ties made of plastic or raffia are useful, but for rose hedging you can also opt for ties made from willow, which are effective and decorative at the same time. Whatever ties you use, check them periodically to make sure that they don't become too tight as the branches grow. Try not to tie one branch to another as friction wounds can occur when branches touch and are rubbed together in the wind.

Buying roses

If you dream of creating a beautiful rose garden make sure you won't be disappointed in a few years' time by considering the size and aspect of your plot, and the size, flowering and growing habits of the roses you choose ... before you buy.

Choose quality plants

Don't always go for the cheapest roses. If you can afford it, it's better to pay for good quality plants that will endure and bring you pleasure for the next ten or twenty years. Buy from a nursery, a garden centre or a reputable rose-specialist mail order catalogue. Roses are generally sold in containers or with bare roots packaged in polythene, although they are also supplied pre-packaged in boxes or with the root ball contained in net or hessian.

Container-grown roses

The best time to plant roses is between late autumn and early spring, but they can be planted any time of year, unless the ground is waterlogged or frozen, or there is a drought. The advantage of buying them during the growing season, when they are in flower, is that you can see exactly what you are buying. Container-grown plants also tend to establish more quickly. However, they are also normally more expensive and the choice of varieties may be limited.

Bare-root roses

These are usually sold by mail order and are normally available during the planting season, i.e. between end autumn and early spring. They should be planted as soon as possible after buying, provided the ground is not frozen, but preferably before the beginning of March. Don't buy plants that appear to have dried out or have started developing thin shoots prematurely, due to being kept in conditions that are too warm. If you cannot plant them out immediately, store them in a cool place such as a shed or garage, where they will be away from danger of frost and keep the roots moist. Alternatively, heel them in (see centre right).

Pre-packaged roses

Sold with their roots in a ball of soil in net or hessian and wrapped in polythene, these roses are often found in outlets such as supermarkets. As the new roots, which can start growing as early as January, are protected by the soil ball, the trauma of transplanting is lessened. These roses can be stored in a cool place (out of danger of frost) to be planted later. Don't buy any plants that appear to have dried out or have started developing thin shoots prematurely.

Heeling-in

If you are not able to plant your roses immediately, heel them into a spare piece of ground. Dig a shallow trench and fill it with peat or sand. Place the roses at an angle in the trench so that the base is supported and cover the roots and base of the stem with loose soil. The grafting or budding point (the scarred pad between the stems and the roots) should be 4–5cm (1½–2in) below the surface. Tamp the soil down so the plants are secure and keep the roots moist.

Choosing a healthy rose

■ Look for a rose with at least two or three healthy stems. They should be green, shiny and unwrinkled (the health of the stems is more important than the number of them). Any buds should be dormant – reject plants already in bud. Foliage on container-grown plants should be vigorous; avoid yellow leaves. Check the rose is not pot bound by sliding it out of the pot; reject any with dense and compacted roots.
■ Examine the roots carefully. To transplant well, a rose should have a well-developed root system with one principal root and lots of smaller roots making a sizeable network, in proportion to the top-growth.

Buying by mail order

1 Clearly, if you buy from a catalogue, there's no possibility of examining the plant first. To minimise the likelihood of any problems, always buy from a reputable and established grower.

2 If you want to be certain that your choice of plants is still available, send in your order as early as possible in the season – in some cases even as early as June for plants to be delivered in November.

3 Call the supplier to ask for an approximate delivery date so that you can have the ground prepared in good time.

4 If possible, plant out your roses as soon they arrive. If this is not possible, heel them in, or store them in a cool place free from frost and keep the roots moist.

What is rootstock?

A rootstock is a root and stem onto which part of another plant (called the 'scion') is grafted (joined). The two become one living plant (the cultivar), the flowering scion drawing strength from the rootstock. In the case of the Standard Rose, a Bush Rose is grafted onto a long straight stem.

When buying a Standard Rose, the rootstock tends to be neglected in favour of the foliage and blooms, yet it's important to know what stock it comes from, if only so that you can choose one that's suited to your soil.

Grafts onto *Rosa multiflora* stock are usually more vigorous in the first year, although their lifespan is shorter. Another disadvantage is that they do not grow well in chalky soil or in a cold climate.

Roses grafted onto *Rosa laxa* Hort. or *Rosa canina* stock are suitable for heavy, chalky soils and produce very few suckers.

■ Unfortunately, very few nurseries indicate the rootstock, so you may find this information difficult to obtain.

■ You should be aware that the same variety can be grown on different stock by different rose-growers. So ask plenty of questions when you buy, to make sure you are aware of all the facts.

Planting

If you're a beginner, you may find it hard to believe that a little clump of sticks you are planting in your border will one day become a beautiful rose bush.

The best soil

Roses are happiest in soil with a good clay content, preferably in full sun, but sheltered from strong winds. For chalky soils, with a pH* of more than 7, add some peat before planting. Acid soils can be improved by adding lime before planting, a process which should be repeated each year. However, a high lime content is harmful. A pH of 7 will guarantee a neutral soil in which roses will thrive. *The pH rating measures the soil's acidity or alkalinity; soil testing kits are available.

Preparing the planting hole

Dig a hole approximately 40–50cm (16–20in) in both width and depth, making sure it is big enough for the roots and deep enough so that the bud union (the bulge at the base of the stem) is about 3-4cm (1½–3in) below ground level. Mix two or three handfuls of dampened peat and a handful of bone meal. Drop into the hole and mix with the soil at the bottom.

Spacing

When planting more than one rose, their size at maturity determines the amount of space you should leave between them. As a guide, for roses with large single blooms or cluster flowers, leave a gap of about 50cm (20in). Allow 60cm (24in) between repeat flowering hybrids and varieties known for vigorous growth. Bush Roses grow fast and should be spaced 80–100cm (2ft 6in–3ft) apart.

Planting a Climber or Rambler

A Climbing Rose should never be planted less than 30cm (12ins) from a wall. Soil at the base of a wall is often poor and dry, but can be improved by adding manure or fertiliser in granular form. Position the plant at an angle, leaning towards the wall with the roots sloping away from the wall. Fix a trellis or a horizontal network of wires across the wall for support.

Planting in a tub

When planting in a pot or tub, make sure there is adequate drainage by placing a handful of gravel at the bottom. Ensure the container is large enough, at least 30–45cm (12–18in) deep for Bush Roses, or 22–35cm (9–14in) for Miniature Roses, and fill with soil-based compost. Feed the plants regularly with fertiliser (see page 22). This is essential as the nutrients in the compost become exhausted over time.

Planting a Standard Rose

Standards need a stake to support them. Treat the base with a wood preservative. Dig and prepare the planting hole as already described (left), then position the stake firmly in the hole, i.e. before you plant the rose. Attach the rose to the stake with ties.

Professional tips

■ To avoid 'soil sickness' which causes poor and stunted growth, never plant a rose bush where one has already been growing. If you have no alternative, it is essential to replace the soil in which the previous rose was grown with fresh soil or a suitable compost.
■ Before planting out a container-grown rose bush, let it soak in a bucket of water for ten minutes before removing the pot. Then plant it without breaking the ball of soil around the roots.

Preparing and planting

1   Before planting, prune all the stems by about 2.5–5 cm (1–2in), making sure any leaves, hips or buds are removed.

2   Place the rose in the centre of the hole and gently spread out the roots. If they are clustered together, position the rose to one side and gently tease them out so they are not in a tight clump.

3   Position the rose so that the budding union is 3–4cm (1½–2in) below the soil. This will ensure the rose is well seated and able to withstand the worst frosts. It will also help limit the growth of suckers.

4   Half-fill the hole with soil, then shake the rose gently to get rid of any air pockets between the roots. Tamp the soil down, then finish filling the hole, adding two handfuls of peat mixed in with the soil.

5   Tamp it down again. Make a shallow basin in the soil around the base of the plant and water thoroughly. The basin will help prevent the water from trickling away.

Feeding and watering

Fertilise your roses well, but don't overdo it – follow the manufacturer's instructions. It is important to add a mixture of moistened peat and bone meal to the soil when planting, but some well-rotted manure or your own household compost will also do the trick.

At spring pruning

Before the leaves are fully open, feed each plant at the base using a specially formulated rose fertiliser. Make sure you follow the manufacturer's instructions – too much will scorch the roots.

As summer starts

A second application of fertiliser can be made in June or July – this will encourage flower growth.

For roses in containers

Roses are quick to take nutrients from the soil, so the soil in a container soon becomes exhausted. Feeding container-grown roses regularly is the key to success. Top-dress the soil with a suitable rose fertiliser at least twice a year (i.e. spread a thin layer of fertiliser on the soil and rake it in lightly).

Different types of fertiliser

■ Fertiliser is available in liquid or soluable form, or in powder or granular form. Always follow the manufacturer's instructions.

■ Spraying liquid feed onto the leaves is known as foliar feeding and is generally regarded as a supplementary feed, not a replacement for another feed. The leaves are fed directly, bypassing the roots. Only do this when the weather is dry.

■ Household compost is made up of recycled organic waste, which produces a natural fertiliser. When using compost, remember that, although it looks like soil, when it has broken down it is actually a feed, and therefore needs to be mixed with soil before being applied. When you are ready to plant a rose, mix some household compost with soil and add a little bone meal and place several handfuls of this mixture at the bottom of the planting hole. To fertilise roses that are already established, put a few handfuls of compost around the base of the plant at the end of winter, and lightly rake it into the soil.

Composting tips

Waste breaks down into compost faster if you layer it, alternating layers of dry waste (straw, twigs, etc.) with damp waste (lawn clippings, kitchen waste, etc). If the waste is in small pieces, it breaks down faster still, so chop up your kitchen waste. Use a garden shredder for small branches, or cut them up by hand.

Water at the base

It is essential to water roses when you plant them to give the plants a good start. Always water roses at the base, since any moisture on the leaves will encourage mildew infection (to which some varieties are prone). Watering should be done at the end of the day, when there is less chance of evaporation caused by the heat of the sun.

Watering in summer

Roses need plenty of water in summer, when the weather is dry, especially if the soil is chalky or sandy. Water generously twice a week, soaking the soil around the roots thoroughly. Don't water little and often as this will encourage the roots to grow closer to the surface. Water container-grown roses on alternate days or every day if the weather is really hot. Roses love the sun but are happiest when their roots are kept cool. Mulching (see page 27) benefits the rose by helping keep the soil cool in summer.

How to make compost

The following method will produce good compost in about three months.

1 Choose a place where you can pile up all your organic waste from the garden and the kitchen. Along with grass clippings, potato peel, apple peel (almost any vegetable waste can be used), good composting items include used coffee filters, cardboard egg boxes, eggshells and wood ash. Avoid cuttings from roses as these can carry disease and don't use cooked food, meat or citrus fruits.

2 Once the pile has started to build up, spread it out in a layer about 30cm (12in) deep over an area measuring about 1 x 2m (3 x 6ft). Dampen it with a commercial compost activator added to water.

3 Repeat the process, and when you have built up four or five layers, cover it over with a thick sheet of black plastic. Remove the plastic after five days or so and turn the heap with a fork to let the air get in, which will help speed it up. Replace the plastic cover, but keep turning the heap periodically.

Natural willow ties

White willow (*Salix alba*) and crack willow (*Salix fragilis*) will both provide excellent natural and flexible ties, but to ensure a plentiful supply, the stems need to be cut back hard, almost to ground level, each year. Other varieties, which are also highly decorative, include common osier or basket-willow (*Salix viminalis*), almond-leaved willow (*Salix triandra*), purple willow (*Salix purpurea*) and grey willow (*Salix cinerea*).

Training Climbing Roses

Climbers or Ramblers need to be trained against supports to ensure they grow in the desired direction. To train a rose against a wall, spread the main branches out in a fan shape, encouraging them to curve. If the principal stems are allowed to grow vertically, the foliage and flowers will tend to be concentrated at the top of the plant.

Training roses around a pergola or pillar

Train the stems around the support and attach with ties (not too tight to allow for growth of the stem). Train young stems in the direction of their natural growth, twisting the main shoots around the support to encourage the formation of flowering shoots lower down.

A little effort for a lot of pleasure

With roses a little care and attention goes a long way, but every rose-lover has to go through the initiation test of getting his or her hands scratched a few times. No pain, no gain... With roses the odd scratch is inevitable – unmarked hands are a sure sign of uncared-for roses!

1
What are suckers?

Cultivated roses are produced by grafting a bush rose onto a rootstock (see page 19). The scar tissue that forms on the rootstock where the graft has been inserted makes a characteristic bulge between the stems and the roots and is known as the grafting point or budding union. With some varieties, suckers (vigorous stems) grow below the bud union on the rootstock itself.

2
Removing suckers

Suckers should be removed as soon as they appear. The term 'sucker' describes just what they do – they suck strength from the rootstock, depriving the cultivar of nourishment. Suckers are usually easy to recognise as the stems are often lighter in colour and the thorns and foliage are usually different from those of the cultivar. To remove them, scrape away the soil just below the grafting point to uncover the base of the sucker. Wearing a pair of gloves, pull the sucker away from the rootstock at the base. Don't cut it off, as this will have the same effect as pruning and will only encourage new sucker shoots to grow.

3
Don't forget to dead-head

The process of dead-heading flowers when they have faded is all too often overlooked. Yet for a number of varieties (Hybrid teas and Floribundas particularly), it is this process that stimulates the development of young shoots and so ensures continuous flowering. If a hip or seed pod is formed once the petals have fallen, remove these also, unless you want to retain them for decorative purposes. Stop dead-heading by the time autumn arrives, or there is the risk of damage from an early frost to the new shoots that are encouraged as a result.

4
Tips on dead-heading

When dead-heading Hybrid Teas (large-flowered roses), make the cut two or three leaf shoots down from the dead head, just above a new bud or fully formed shoot. Always make a slanting cut, on the opposite side from the new bud or shoot. Follow the same process for roses with clusters of flowers (trusses). If some blooms in the centre of the truss fade first, cut those off individually and then remove the whole truss when all the blooms have faded.

5
Hip-bearing roses

A number of Shrub Roses develop beautiful rosehips when their petals have fallen. If you leave them on the stem they will make a lovely display after flowering is over and the gesture might also be appreciated by the local birds – but if you decide to cut them off you might feel tempted to make some jam.

6
Rosehip jelly

For this recipe, use the hips from either a wild rose or one of the *Rugosas*.

Take 2.5 kilos (about 5lb) of ripe rosehips. Boil two litres (4pts) of water and then add the hips. Cook for 15 minutes then strain through a coarse vegetable strainer. Strain the rosehips again for a second time, using a finer strainer, then a third time, using a very fine strainer or a jelly bag. Put the resulting purée into a pan, add sugar (allowing 800g per kilo of pulp or 1¾ lb per 2lb), and simmer for 15 minutes, stirring continuously. Check the consistency of the jelly by spooning a little onto a chilled saucer. If it's too runny, continue to simmer and test until it has thickened sufficiently. Transfer the jelly into pots and put the lids on while it is still hot. Keep turning the pots until the jelly is completely cool.

Weeding and applying mulch

Unfortunately, the appearance of weeds among your prize roses is inevitable, but here are a few tips to help save both time and effort.

Remove all roots

Make sure that you clear the soil of all weeds and roots before planting. Even the most spindly and innocuous-looking roots can develop into pernicious perennial weeds such as bindweed or ground elder. Once installed, they are hard to eradicate and can also become tangled with the roots of the rose.

Preventive weeding

Weed around the base of a Ground-cover Rose before it has had a chance to spread too far. Ground-cover Roses will normally suppress the growth of weeds due to their spreading habit, but the ground over which they spread should be cleared of weeds first.

In the spring

When spring arrives, it is certain that many of the first shoots to peep through the soil in your garden will belong to weeds. Tackle them without delay, before the roots start to penetrate the soil deeply, making them harder to pull up. If you don't dig them up as soon as you spot them, at least make sure you remove them before they have time to run to seed and propagate new weeds. Don't put weeds on the compost heap where they may take hold and thrive. Instead, burn them or dispose of them at a local refuse site.

When to apply mulch?

Mulching is the name given to the practice of placing a layer of organic (normally) material on the surface of the soil to suppress the growth of weeds. It should be carried out when the soil has begun to warm up but still retains some moisture, generally around April, depending on the climate in your region.

Preparing the soil for mulching

Dig over the soil thoroughly and remove all traces of weeds and unidentifiable roots. Remove surface debris, such as dead leaves, twigs, etc. and if the soil is dry, water it. Apply the spring feed (see page 22) before the mulch.

Choosing mulch

Mulch can be made from leaf mould, well-rotted manure or garden compost; chipped bark and cocoa bean shells also work well. Alternatively a simple layer of moistened peat can be used. Some people use a layer of plastic sheeting (decidedly not organic), but since this looks unattractive, it is best covered with a layer of chipped bark or cocoa bean shells. If you opt for straw, make sure there are no seeds left in it, as these will start to grow quickly. A layer of mulch should be around 10cm (4in) thick.

Making your own mulch

■ Lawn clippings can be used provided they have started to rot down (dry lawn clippings can be flammable). They are best used in large rose beds and not in a polyantha border. Do not use lawn clippings if a weedkiller has recently been used on the lawn, or if the lawn contains weeds.

■ If you have a garden shredder, use this to make your own wood chippings from twigs and branches.

■ Beware of using ash from the fireplace. It has high potassium and makes water penetration difficult.

Advantages of mulching

1	Mulching reduces the workload considerably. It is recommended for any gardener who is short of time or often away from home.
2	The need for watering is reduced, since mulch lessens the rate of evaporation.
3	Mulching helps to keep the soil at a cool and even temperature.
4	The soil remains light and aerated, because mulching prevents it from becoming too compacted by heavy rain.
5	Not only a valuable ally in the struggle to keep weeds at bay, mulching is also an excellent means of enriching the soil.

Treating pests and diseases

Systemic insecticides are absorbed into plant tissues and spread through the plant via the sap, killing any insects that suck the sap. Contact insecticides kill when sprayed on insects. Contact fungicides can kill spores about to germinate, but are not so effective on established fungal diseases. Systemic fungicides kill fungal diseases in the plant tissues. Treat any attack as soon as you spot it, spraying the top and underside of leaves thoroughly. Don't spray in the wind or hot sun. Don't leave rose debris such as leaves and twigs lying on the ground, it could spread disease. Burn it or dispose of it safely, but don't put it on the compost heap.

Rust and rose black spot

Both rust and rose black spot can occur when the weather is hot and humid.

Rust shows itself in the form of orange pustules on the underside of leaves, normally around July. The pustules eventually turn black and can affect the leaf stalks also. Remove all diseased leaves and stalks (and burn them) and spray with a suitable fungicide as soon as possible. Repeat-spray every two weeks until the plant is clear.

Black spot manifests itself in spots or patches on the leaves, which eventually turn yellow and drop off. Remove all infected leaves and burn them. If black spot attacks, spray with a fungicide, but the most effective treatment is to use a preventive fungicidal spray every two weeks between June and September. When removing diseased leaves, make sure to remove any leaves that have fallen on the ground since the disease can remain dormant in the soil until the following season.

If treating a rose during winter, an application of Bordeaux mixture (a fungicide) will destroy the spores connected with these diseases.

Powdery mildew

This is another disease that frequently affects roses. The main symptom is a whitish, powdery coating that appears on both leaves and buds. The leaves become distorted and fall early. If left untreated, this fungal infection spreads rapidly, and weakens plants to the point where they can no longer come into bloom. Remove affected areas and burn them, and spray with a fungicide.

Greenfly

Greenfly love roses bushes, and feed on them by sucking their sap through new shoots. As a preventative measure, spray with a systemic insecticide, which is drawn through the leaves into the sap. However, if a colony of greenfly has already installed itself, use a contact insecticide to kill them off – make sure you wet the entire plant.

Caterpillars

Commercial sprays can be used on caterpillars, but unless their numbers are completely unmanageable, it is easy enough to remove them by hand . . . or leave it to the birds. Erect nesting boxes in the autumn and by the spring, tits should be making short work of the caterpillars.

Thrips and red spider mites

Thrips are tiny flies that leave the edges of leaves and petals spotted with tiny black dots, distorting the flowers or preventing them from opening. They can also cause white flecking on petals. Red spider mites cause leaves to become dull and discolour, turning bronze. A fine white webbing often appears on the underside of the leaves. Treat attacks with a suitable insecticide as soon as the first symptoms appear.

Organic treatments

■ If you want to be completely 'green' and forego any chemicals, one option is to introduce ladybirds into the garden. These are available by mail order as well as from certain specialist shops. Release them between May and mid-August and they will soon polish off greenfly as well as produce copious quantities of larvae that will be equally ravenous.

■ Nettle manure is another alternative solution for combating greenfly. Use about one kilo (2lb) of young nettles (ones that have not gone to seed) to 10 litres (two-and-a-half gallons) of rainwater or spring water. Leave to steep in the water for 4–5 days. Then dilute with five parts water and apply by spraying.

Pruning

There is a great deal of debate about the 'thorny' subject of pruning, but you just need to follow a few simple rules. Pruning stimulates the growth of new shoots and removes dead wood while giving the rose bush a pleasing shape.

Vital equipment

■ A pair of thick gloves is essential, to protect against thorns.
■ Make sure that your secateur blades are sharp. Some gardeners recommend playing safe and disinfecting the blades after every plant, in order not to spread disease.
■ A pair of pruning loppers and a pruning saw will prove indispensable when it comes to removing any thicker branches.

Pruning hints

1   Prune roses just above a bud that is beginning to swell. If you are pruning early in the year, buds may not always be easy to recognise – look for them just above a leaf scar.

2   In order to avoid a tangle of stems and enable air to circulate freely within the bush, it is advisable to make the cut above a bud that faces towards the outside of the plant, rather than towards the inside, enabling the bud to develop into an outward-facing shoot.

3   The cut should be made diagonally across the stem, so that the slope runs away from (rather than towards) the bud. This is to avoid allowing water to run down the slope and collect in the angle of the bud and the stem, causing the bud to rot.

4   Don't cut too close to or too far from the bud, leave about 1cm ($\frac{1}{2}$in) of stem above the bud.

5   Apart from single flowering roses, which are pruned after they have flowered, pruning is normally carried out when the rose is dormant or semi-dormant, i.e. during the period after the leaves have fallen in autumn and before spring. It is usually carried out in spring, just as the buds are beginning to swell, but before the leaves have appeared. Roses can pruned during the growing season, but growth will be severely checked.

Step-by-step pruning

The following rules apply to established plants, or those that were planted at least 12 months ago. For newly-planted roses, see page 34.

Bush Roses *(see page 34)*

Bush Roses should be pruned at the end of February or in March. However, it is advisable to cut back long stems by about one third in the autumn to avoid damage caused by strong winds and to improve the general appearance.

1 First, remove any dead wood, along with any weak stems or stems that cross one another.

2 All the remaining sound and healthy stems should then be cut back to about 20cm (8in) from the ground. This fairly hard pruning will encourage the growth of attractive, well-shaped blooms, although there will be fewer than with a lighter prune.

Floribunda, or cluster-flowering roses and Miniature Roses

Prune Floribunda and Miniature Roses in spring only moderately, by cutting back the main stems by about one-third of their length.

Shrub Roses *(see page 34)*

Some Shrub Roses can reach a quite considerable size. Prune late February/March.

1 Remove weak or dead stems and any branches or stems that cross one another.

2 Identify and distinguish between the main branches which make up the framework of the plant and the secondary branches or stems. The main branches produce the most growth. Remove the oldest of these main branches and cut back the remaining ones by about one-third, allowing enough space for the flowers to bloom well.

3 The secondary stems that grow from the main branches should be cut back to two or three buds from the base.

Standard Roses

Standard Roses consist of a cultivar grafted onto the stem of another rose.

1 In spring, remove all weak or dead wood.

2 Prune the remaining stems only moderately, cutting back by about one-third of the total length, in order to maintain an attractive shape. Cut the stems just above an outward-facing bud (as described on page 31).

Weeping Standards

Weeping Standards are Climbers grafted onto the stem of another rose and are mostly single flowering. They should be pruned after flowering. Cut back each stem that has flowered. Again, the aim is to maintain a balanced look by shortening the longest branches, which are also susceptible to winter winds.

Single flowering roses

Prune roses that flower just once in the summer moderately, after they have finished flowering. Pruning stimulates the growth of side shoots on which the following season's buds will appear.

1 Begin by removing any dead wood and weak branches, cutting them off at the base.

2 Do the same with any stems or branches that cross one another – disease can take hold in the wounds caused by branches rubbing together.

3 Now prune the remaining stems, making your cut above a bud. The side stems should also be cut back, but without losing sight of the overall shape.

Climbing Roses *(see page 35)*

1 For the first two years after planting, Climbing Roses need no pruning at all, just make sure that the branches are trained around the supports as you require. Spread the branches out as far as possible in a horizontal direction – it is from these main horizontal branches that the lateral branches will grow, on which the flower buds will develop.

2 From the third year after planting onwards, in early spring, cut back any dead wood.

3 Any weak-looking branches should be cut back to the first bud, to encourage a new stem to grow. If a vigorous, healthy shoot has already begun growing, cut off the weak stem to just above the healthy one.

4 All the side shoots should then be cut back to half their length, to encourage flowering.

Rambling Roses and Ground-cover Roses

Little pruning is required other than to bring them back under control if they have spread too far, to remove dead wood and generally tidy them up. Prune Ground-cover Roses in the spring and Rambling Roses once they have finished flowering.

Rose arches

Arches are a popular way to encourage single flowering roses to bloom more productively and over a longer period.

1   For the course of a whole summer growing season, allow new shoots to grow without pruning, from old wood that has flowered.

2   In January or February of the following year, bend the new branches over the arch, attaching them at the ends to the framework of the arch. This has the effect of slowing down the circulation of the sap within the rose, and enables the branch to flower along its whole length.

3   The following year the oldest branches can be removed, and a fresh arch created out of the new wood.

4   If repeated every year, this will benefit those varieties with a very short flowering season.

Basic principles of pruning

Trimming a rose before planting

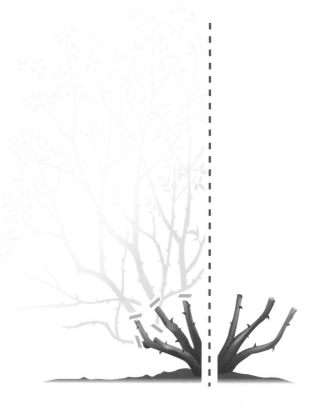

Pruning an established Bush Rose

Newly-planted roses

All newly-planted roses (those that
were planted in the spring or were
planted the previous autumn or winter)
should be cut back hard, irrespective
of type, to about 12-15cm (5-6ins)
above the soil. This stimulates growth
and encourages new shoots to grow
from close to the base.

Roses planted in the autumn should
not be pruned until spring.

Roses planted in February or March
should be pruned at the outset.

*For pruning established roses, see
page 32.*

When to prune

Roses should not be pruned at any
time of the year. Single flowering
varieties should be pruned after they
have flowered, in the summer. All other
varieties should normally be pruned in
the first half of March, or when the
buds are beginning to swell, but leaves
have not yet developed.

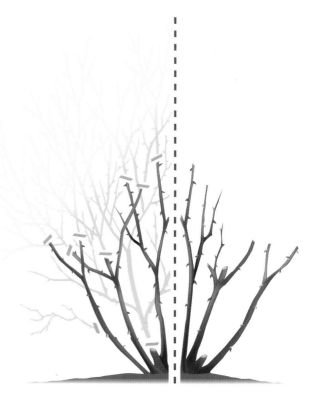

Pruning an established Shrub Rose

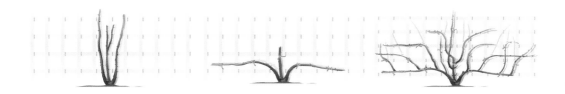

Training and pruning a Climbing Rose in the first three years

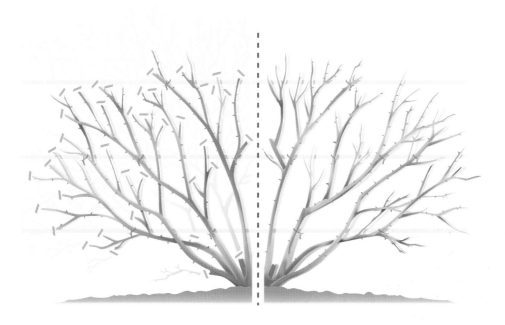

Pruning a repeat flowering Climbing Rose (in early spring)

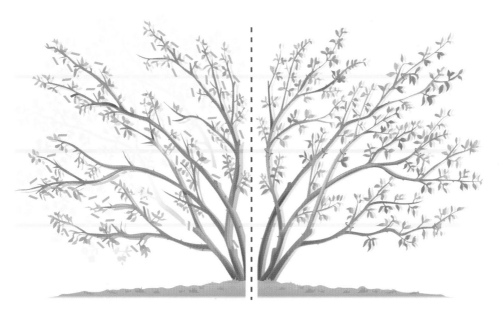

Pruning a single flowering Climbing Rose (after flowering)

Propagation

Propagating your own plants can be immensely satisfying. After all, you are creating new plants for free! There are several techniques, including budding where a bud of one variety is set into the rootstock of another. This is the way most commercial roses are propagated, but is probably best left to the professionals. However, layering and taking cuttings are two methods that the amateur rose grower can use quite easily.

Taking cuttings

This technique is suitable for Shrub Roses, healthy Floribunda, Climbers, Ramblers and Miniature Roses as well as Botanical Roses and old Bush Roses. It is a good idea to take several cuttings at the same time in case some have difficulty in taking root.

Semi-ripe cuttings

In June, select several healthy new shoots (this year's growth) about 6cm (2½in) in length and 5mm (¼in) in width. They should be almost fully grown, and have two to four buds and several sets of leaves.

Cut the shoots off below a bud using a horizontal cut. Then cut off the tops of each shoot above a bud with a slanting cut (leaving the required 6cm (2½in) length). Remove all thorns and strip off any sets of leaves on the lower part of the shoots, but leave two sets at the top. If these are too large, cut them in half. Next, dip the base of the shoots into rooting powder. Prepare some pots with a mixture of sand and moistened peat mixed in equal parts, and bury the cuttings to two-thirds of their length.

Place the pots under some form of protection, such as a propagator or cover them with plastic bags, to keep the humidity at a constant level. Keep an eye on the soil in the pots to make sure it doesn't dry out. Keep them in a shady place.

After about two months, the cuttings should have developed sufficiently to be ready to plant out.

Layering

Spring is a good time to use the layering technique. Most roses with long supple stems that can be bent down to ground level can be layered easily, including Old Roses, such as Damasks, Albas and Bourbons, as well as Climbers and all Ramblers.

Choose a healthy, supple branch that is one year old. Remove the leaves along the section that is to be buried and make a diagonal cut about 2.5cm (1in) long in the side of the branch facing the ground, about 30cm (12in) from the end. Hold the cut open by wedging a matchstick in it.

Dip the cut part in rooting powder and bury it below soil level, pegging it down to hold it in position .

After a few months, once the layered section has started to grow sufficiently it can be separated from the parent plant, but be careful not to do this too early. The layered plant can then be planted out in its final position in the autumn, but take care to keep the root ball intact.

Hardwood cuttings

Most rose varieties can be propagated with this technique.

1   At the beginning of winter, around December, select some healthy, first-year branches that bore flowers in the summer, of about 30cm (12in) in length and around 5mm (¼in) in width.

2   Cut the branches off the plant below a bud, using a horizontal cut. Then cut off the tops of the branches above a bud, using a slanting cut, so that the resulting cutting is about 23cm (9ins) long. Take off the leaves, without removing their stalks.

3   Dip the base of the cuttings into rooting powder.

4   Using a pencil, make some planting holes in an area of fine soil in a sheltered position and place the cuttings in the holes, so that about two thirds of their length is buried. Firm up the soil and water.

5   Alternatively, plant the cuttings in pots, in a mixture of equal parts moistened peat and sand. Put the pots in a sheltered position or under a cold frame, making sure that the soil remains moist.

6   By the following autumn the cuttings should have taken root and can be planted out in their final position, or left to grow for another year. Take care not to damage the roots when lifting them out.

The rose-grower's palette

White represents innocence and purity, red pure passion and yellow conjures up sunlight and sparkle.

But in my heart of hearts I know that I would set aside the best spot of all in my little corner of Paradise for the simple pink innocence of a lovely Old Rose that tugs at the heartstrings.

White roses

'Dupontii'
Gallica hybrid. Before 1817

'Iceberg'
Floribunda. Kordes 1958

Description: This rose has strong branches that grow straight from the centre of the bush and then arch out in a delicate curve. It bears very simple flowers, all white with just a glint of yellow or brown stamens. The flowers open out into clusters and give off a heady fragrance. In autumn, the small, bright orange hips form a lovely contrast with the grey-green foliage.

Position: Since it can tolerate poor soil, this rose will fit in anywhere. Perfect in front of a hedge, it also looks good in a mixed border. Its relatively wild appearance means that it is at its best in a natural, informal setting.

Description: It is hardly surprising that this splendid Floribunda (also known as 'Fée des Neiges', or 'snow fairy') is so widespread in our gardens. Its lightly-scented double flowers are a brilliant, pure white and repeat constantly from early summer through to autumn. This Shrub Rose has an upright stance, and its shiny, dark green foliage has no particular susceptibility to disease.

Position: Often planted in quantity to create a border, or alongside a contrasting box hedge, which enhances its brilliant whiteness, this rose is also spectacular mixed in with perennials such as Lady's Mantle or variegated hostas. The blooms themselves are excellent for cutting and are frequently used in bouquets.

Characteristics
- **Height:** 250cm (8ft)
- **Spread:** 220cm (7ft 6in)
- **Flowering:** single flowering
- **Pruning:** light pruning of the lateral branches after flowering

Characteristics
- **Height:** 90cm (3ft)
- **Spread:** 65cm (26in)
- **Flowering:** repeat flowering
- **Pruning:** normal pruning at the end of winter

'Manning's Blush'
UK before 1799

Rosa fedtschenkoana
Asia 1880

Description: This Shrub Rose has medium-sized flowers that are white with a hint of pink in the centre. The bloom is flat yet full, with a lovely perfume, while the bush has a compact shape and luxuriant foliage that gives off a pleasant green-apple fragrance.

Position: Easy to integrate into a low hedge, this rose also looks good mixed in with perennials, providing them with a solid backdrop. Suitable plants to place in front could include nepetas (catmint) or salvias (flowering sage).

Description: A beautiful Shrub Rose that fits well into a natural garden, where its modest outline blends in perfectly. Its simple flowers are of the purest white, with attractive golden stamens and delicate, slightly crumpled, paper-like petals. The foliage is downy and grey-green in colour. In the autumn, the whole bush is covered with hips that are almost a perfect pear-shape.

Position: An ideal choice to form part of a natural hedge when used with other shrubs or roses of similar appearance, it also looks handsome against a backdrop of hedging plants such as purple-leaf hazel or dogwood.

Characteristics

- **Height:** 120cm (4ft)
- **Spread:** 120cm (4ft)
- **Flowering:** mostly single flowering, but may occasionally repeat flower in autumn
- **Pruning:** remove dead or weak stems; at the end of summer cut back lateral branches that flowered

Characteristics

- **Height:** 150cm (5ft)
- **Spread:** 120cm (4ft)
- **Flowering:** repeat flowering
- **Pruning:** light pruning at the end of winter

White roses

Rosa alba 'Maxima'
Alba. Before 1867

'Prosperity'
Moschata. Pemberton 1919

Description: An alluring combination of large, double creamy-white blooms with a good fragrance that open out into thick clusters and bluish-green foliage. Although it only flowers for a short time, this handsome Shrub Rose regains its splendour in the autumn with a display of decorative oval-shaped hips.

Position: A versatile shrub that looks attractive both on its own or forming part of a hedge. It is set off to good effect alongside other plants that come into bloom at the same time, such as delphiniums.

Description: This dense Shrub Rose with a sprawling habit has attractive, shiny foliage that shows off to perfection its well-formed double roses, which are ivory-white with a lemony-yellow centre. The blooms grow in clusters and have a powerful perfume. The weight of each stem lends a graceful movement to the shrub, giving it additional charm.

Position: Several of these roses planted side by side in borders look superb, although if planted in isolation, the effect would be enhanced by using three plants, placing them in a triangle about 1m (3ft) apart.

Characteristics

- **Height:** 200cm (6ft 6in)
- **Spread:** 150cm (5ft)
- **Flowering:** single flowering, in June
- **Pruning:** after flowering

Characteristics

- **Height:** 150cm (5ft)
- **Spread:** 120cm (4ft)
- **Flowering:** repeat flowering
- **Pruning:** at the end of winter

'Blanc Double de Coubert'
Rugosa. Cochet 1892

'Sombreuil'
Tea Rose. Robert 1850

Description: A vigorous and dense Shrub Rose that is a popular choice due to its large, pure white double blossoms, which are highly fragrant and reminiscent of paper flowers. Typical of the *Rosa rugosa* family, it has honeycombed foliage that is highly resistant to disease. The autumn foliage turns a magnificent golden yellow, and round red hips sometimes appear, although rarely in any quantity.

Position: Useful for creating an informal hedge, this shrub can also be planted as edging or incorporated into a mixed border. It stands firmly upright and looks good with mounds of pink or white geraniums planted at its base.

Description: A dense shrub that can be trained as a low Climber, this rose produces large, double, quartered flowers with the noticeable fragrance that is characteristic of Tea Roses. The overall colour is creamy-white, but it is not unusual for the centre of the bloom to be flushed with tinges of pink, especially just before the petals fall. It is a good-sized plant that will flower until winter sets in.

Position: As is the case with most Tea Roses, 'Sombreuil' is relatively fragile, so it is advisable to give it plenty of winter protection in harsher climates. Attractive grown as a specimen shrub, it is also pretty as a Climber if positioned against a wall or given a little support.

Characteristics

- **Height:** 150cm (5ft)
- **Spread:** 180cm (6ft)
- **Flowering:** repeat flowering
- **Pruning:** cut back the branches by about one-third at the end of winter

Characteristics

- **Height:** 150cm (5ft)
- **Spread:** 150cm (5ft)
- **Flowering:** generous repeat flowering
- **Pruning:** light pruning at the end of winter

Pink roses

'Jacques Cartier'
Portland. Moreau-Robert 1868

'Erfurt'
Kordes 1939

Description: This is a splendid example of a Shrub Rose with strong, double blooms of a pure, brilliant pink, each made up of perfect quarters concealing glimpses of a delicious green centre. There is an abundance of light green foliage. With its rich, strong fragrance this is an excellent rose that is also recommended for cutting.

Position: 'Jacques Cartier' looks beautiful planted as a low hedge or incorporated into a mixed border. Ideal accompaniments are scabious or butterfly lavender. This variety will happily tolerate being grown in a container and has the additional useful quality of being able to tolerate partial shade.

Description: The simple elegance of this modern Shrub Rose together with its long flowering period have earned it a place among the finest varieties. Its cerise-pink flowers become paler towards the centre and have a blissful purity and fragrance. The thick, dark green foliage is carried on gleaming, thorny branches.

Position: 'Erfurt's' highly pleasing appearance and robust strength often earn it a prominent position in the garden. It works well when mixed in with hedging shrubs, or in a prime spot at the back of a bed of perennials.

Characteristics
- **Height:** 120cm (4ft)
- **Spread:** 90cm (3ft)
- **Flowering:** good repeat flowering
- **Pruning:** normal pruning at the end of winter

Characteristics
- **Height:** 150cm (5ft)
- **Spread:** 120cm (4ft)
- **Flowering:** repeat flowering
- **Pruning:** cut back by one-third at the end of winter, keeping a balanced shape

'Félicité Parmentier'
Alba. Parmentier 1834

'Leonardo da Vinci'
Meilland 1994

Description: These flat, fully double flowers have an attractive flesh-pink hue that becomes paler before the blooms die off. The petals have a tendency to curl over as the flower opens, giving the rose its characteristic rounded appearance. This is a well-balanced, bushy shrub – of fairly modest size for a *Rosa alba* – with elegant leaves of a grey-blue tone.

Position: Ideal for creating a low hedge, or possibly planted in front of a row of yews or flowering shrubs, 'Félicité Parmentier' will flower happily even in a semi-shaded spot.

Description: Half Shrub Rose and half *Floribunda*, this rose bush bears nicely rounded, fully double flowers of a pronounced Bengal pink hue. One of the most robust of all varieties, the blooms have good staying power and can even withstand torrential rain. 'Leonardo da Vinci' combines the romantic feel of an Old Rose with the personality of a modern variety.

Position: If using a number of these roses for hedging, where the effect of using several plants together will be most striking, plant them 40cm (16in) apart, either in a straight or a staggered line.

Characteristics

- **Height:** 100cm (39in)
- **Spread:** 90cm (36in)
- **Flowering:** single flowering
- **Pruning:** cut back after flowering, as with most single flowering roses

Characteristics

- **Height:** 80cm (32in)
- **Spread:** 70cm (28in)
- **Flowering:** repeat flowering
- **Pruning:** cut back the branches by about one-third in early spring

Pink roses

'Centenaire de Lourdes'
Floribunda. Delbard-Chabert 1958

'La Ville de Bruxelles'
Damascena. Vibert 1849

Description: It's surprising that this beautiful *Floribunda* is not seen more often in gardens. Generous clusters of semi-double flowers bloom continuously from the beginning of summer through to the autumn. A lovely cerise, with a sprinkling of darker pink, the petals are lightly crumpled at the edges and give off a jasmine fragrance. Two other noteworthy characteristics are that it is easy to grow and that it has plentiful leaf coverage, its shiny, green foliage being very resistant to disease.

Position: Although perfect for growing in a border, with careful pruning 'Centenaire de Lourdes' can be made into a beautiful specimen Shrub Rose for a solo position. It will also thrive happily in a tub or pot.

Characteristics
- **Height:** 120cm (4ft)
- **Spread:** 120cm (4ft)
- **Flowering:** repeat flowering
- **Pruning:** at the end of winter

Description: A vigorous Damask Shrub Rose with an upright stance, valued for its large, double quartered flowers of a crisp pink hue, which open out in clusters supported on strong, straight stems. The powerful fragrance that it produces is delicious.

Position: Used to great effect when planted singly, this rose can also look stunning when planted in a triangular group of three, with a gap of 80–100cm (32–39in) between each plant. If planted in a border, the fresh colour of this rose is set off attractively by white roses or by gypsophila.

Characteristics
- **Height:** 130cm (4ft 4in)
- **Spread:** 100cm (3ft 3in)
- **Flowering:** single flowering
- **Pruning:** after flowering

'Camaïeu'
Gallica. Vibert 1830

'Fêtes Galantes'
Delbard 1994

Description: With colouring reminiscent of 'Variegata di Bologna', this is an opulent and sensuous rose. Its medium-sized blooms are elegant in shape and richly perfumed, presenting a profusion of pale carmine double petals, striped through with crimson and a spectrum of purples. The flowers grow on a compact shrub with profuse foliage.

Position: Equally effective in a low hedge or grown in a container, this rose can also be incorporated into a border. Its unpredictable flowering season can present difficulties if planted alongside other perennials with a short flowering season.

Description: Devotees of the classic Hybrid Teas will not be disappointed by this flawless rose which produces blooms of great quality. Its fragrant flowers are supremely elegant and will appeal greatly to lovers of perfume. A healthy, vigorous bush which produces a profusion of flowers.

Position: Planted in a large bed, this rose can be happily set alongside lavender or a big artemisia (e.g. 'Powis Castle'), where it will soon form a vigorous and solid mass of colour that is both vivid and long-lasting.

Characteristics
- **Height:** 90cm (3ft)
- **Spread:** 90cm (3ft)
- **Flowering:** single flowering
- **Pruning:** after flowering

Characteristics
- **Height:** 90cm (3ft)
- **Spread:** 90cm (3ft)
- **Flowering:** repeat flowering
- **Pruning:** prune to two or three buds at the end of winter

Pink roses

'Comte de Chambord'
Portland. Moreau-Robert 1863

'Auberge de l'Ill'
Eve 2002

Description: This Old Rose is very similar to 'Jacques Cartier' – so much so that it was impossible to decide between them for inclusion here. It produces fully double blooms, often quartered and a crisp pink in colour, dotted with hints of lilac. It gives off a strong, heady perfume. The foliage is a soft green, with sizeable leaves growing on erect stems that are profusely thorny.

Position: Ideal for small spaces, the attractive appearance of this rose will be displayed to good effect in a kitchen garden or a small, enclosed garden. It works particularly well set among irises and peonies.

Description: Expert rose-grower André Eve is justifiably proud of this creation. A bush of generous proportions, it has an abundance of branches and produces large, explosive clusters of delicate, pale pink pompons that bloom continuously all summer and well into autumn. Extremely reliable and easy to grow, it also offers excellent resistance to disease.

Position: A versatile rose that is suitable for a number of different locations, it works well at the front of a bed or border or at the edge of a pond. Its jolly appearance makes it ideal for brightening up the entrance to a kitchen garden, although it also produces a marvellous display on a terrace or balcony, thanks to its profuse and long-lasting flowering period.

Characteristics

- **Height:** 90cm (3ft)
- **Spread:** 60cm (2ft)
- **Flowering:** good repeat flowering
- **Pruning:** normal pruning at the end of winter

Characteristics

- **Height:** about 50cm (20in)
- **Spread:** 50cm (20in)
- **Flowering:** repeat flowering
- **Pruning:** normal pruning at the end of winter

'Gloire des Mousseux'
Centifolia Muscosa. Laffay 1852

'Celestial'
Alba. 1797

Description: An Old Rose that truly epitomises sensuousness. Its generous, large, double blooms are a gentle shade of pink that is at once bright and delicate. Its strong perfume will delight even the least sensitive nose with a delicious fragrance that is soft and slightly fruity. A robust shrub, its foliage is bright green with an attractive mossing.

Position: Equally decorative by itself or forming part of a hedge, this rose can also be grown quite happily in a container. For this reason, it is almost *de rigueur* to choose it for your balcony or terrace.

Description: The uniform pale pink of 'Celestial's' semi-double blooms makes a handsome contrast with its golden stamens. Pretty, spiral-shaped buds fill the surrounding air with a beautiful, gentle perfume. This is a vigorous shrub with grey-blue foliage that remains disease-free.

Position: This Shrub Rose is suitable for use in hedges and mixed borders. If a short flowering season puts you off, it is worth bearing in mind that there are plenty of good ways of giving a new lease of life to single flowering roses – just add clematis or perhaps a climbing annual such as Morning Glory. It will also tolerate partial shade.

Characteristics
- **Height:** 130cm (4ft 3in)
- **Spread:** 100cm (39in)
- **Flowering:** single flowering
- **Pruning:** cut back by about one-third after flowering

Characteristics
- **Height:** 150cm (5ft)
- **Spread:** 120cm (4ft)
- **Flowering:** single flowering
- **Pruning:** after flowering

Red roses

'William Shakespeare 2000'
David Austin 2000

'Charles de Mills'
Gallica. Before 1790

Description: It is easy to see why this rose from well-known specialist rose-grower David Austin has everyone reaching for superlatives, because it really is splendid. For those who like their roses deep crimson with velvety petals, this is a good find. Upright in habit, with generous foliage, its blooms have an exceptional fragrance, making it one of the finest English roses in the dark red category.

Position: This relatively low-growing rose bush will suit the front of a mixed bed. It has good repeat flowering, making it very popular for low hedging.

Description: These magnificent roses are very large, with a purplish crimson hue that takes on a lilac sheen as the flower matures. The rounded buds open up into shallow, flat-topped blooms divided into quarters. This thick, vigorous shrub has branches that soon lose their early straightness and develop an attractive, arching habit. Also known by its old name 'Bizarre Triomphant', its origins are unknown but it is certainly one of the loveliest Gallic roses.

Position: Perfect for hedging, this rose can also be used in borders. Its deep colour makes a wonderful contrast with purple and blue sage, or against a backdrop of Brazilian verbena.

Characteristics
- **Height:** 100cm (39in)
- **Spread:** 80cm (32in)
- **Flowering:** repeat flowering
- **Pruning:** remove about one-third of each branch after the last frost

Characteristics
- **Height:** 120cm (4ft)
- **Spread:** 100cm (39in)
- **Flowering:** single flowering
- **Pruning:** cut back the side branches after flowering

'Tuscany Superb'
Gallica. Rivers 1837

'Henri Martin'
Centifolia Muscosa. Laffay 1863

Description: This is an exceptional Gallic rose. Each flower opens out into a deep bowl of velvety petals that are a sumptuous crimson with hints of purple, and larger and more profuse than those of 'Tuscany', which is rarely seen nowadays. The very fragrant, semi-double blooms are carried on a dense bush with an upright habit.

Position: A variety that is ideal for growing in hedges incorporated with other roses, or among flowering shrubs. It also works well as the focal point of a mixed border.

Description: This beautiful Moss Rose has double blooms of a strong crimson, revealing glimpses of beautiful golden stamens. 'Henri Martin' flowers only once per season, which is reason enough to take full advantage of the splendid show it puts on when in full bloom. A bush with an upright stance, it has foliage that is light in colour showing off the deep tone of the flowers to good effect.

Position: For anyone with an eye for a romantic setting, this is a gorgeous rose, whether grown by itself or as part of a mixed border. It also looks fabulous grown on a frame or support.

Characteristics

- **Height:** 120cm (4ft)
- **Spread:** 100cm (39in)
- **Flowering:** single flowering
- **Pruning:** light pruning after flowering

Characteristics

- **Height:** 180cm (6ft)
- **Spread:** 120cm (4ft)
- **Flowering:** single flowering
- **Pruning:** after flowering

Red roses

'Le Rouge et le Noir'
Delbard 1973

'William Lobb'
Centifolia Muscosa. Laffay 1855

Description: Another of Delbard's splendid creations, its superb, large, well-formed double flowers have petals of a deep red hue, edged with tinges of sensuous black, hence its name in French. As if that were not enough, it has a wonderful perfume of roses mixed with vanilla, as well as first-class resistance to disease. The foliage is shiny and dark green in colour.

Position: The perfect rose for a border, it is also very popular for use in bouquets, its exquisite flowers have long stems and are easy to handle.

Description: 'William Lobb's' large, flat, double flowers are highly mossy and grow in clusters at the end of powerful, long, arching stems. The colour is quite exceptional − a crimson-purple with glints of mauve. Although a Moss Rose, only the buds and flower stalks are mossy, but the flowers give off an excellent perfume.

Position: A vigorous, large shrub, it needs a solid support. If planted as part of a hedge, its branches can rely on support from the surrounding bushes. It can also be persuaded to climb if it is trained against a wall or up a pillar.

Characteristics

- **Height:** 90cm (3ft)
- **Spread:** 90cm (3ft)
- **Flowering:** repeat flowering
- **Pruning:** prune to two or three buds at the end of winter

Characteristics

- **Height:** 180cm (6ft)
- **Spread:** 150cm (5ft)
- **Flowering:** single flowering
- **Pruning:** light pruning after flowering

'Cardinal de Richelieu'
Gallica. Laffay 1840

'Mrs Anthony Waterer'
Rugosa. Waterer 1898

Description: Beautifully-shaped, fully double flowers of a subtle purple laced with violet are borne on slender stems that are almost thorn-free. A compact shrub with dense, healthy, light green foliage, it makes a stunning display in June. Although this rose is not remarkable for its fragrance, there is some perfume present.

Position: An ideal choice for creating a hedge of medium height, 'Cardinal de Richelieu' is equally suited to planting in a mixed border. Plant an orange *hemerocallis*, (or daylily) nearby for an interesting tonal combination.

Description: 'Mrs Anthony Waterer' is an Old Rose that bears a profusion of semi-double flowers that are a deep shade of red and pleasantly perfumed. The bush is a vigorous grower with strong, thorny branches covered by handsome, dark green foliage.

Position: Like all the *Rugosa* family, this variety is ideal when used in hedging. It has an attractive shape − more so than many − which also makes it good for cultivation in a solo position on a lawn.

Characteristics

- **Height:** 120cm (4ft)
- **Spread:** 100cm (39in)
- **Flowering:** single flowering
- **Pruning:** light pruning after flowering

Characteristics

- **Height:** 150cm (5ft)
- **Spread:** 150cm (5ft)
- **Flowering:** in June, with a reasonable repeat flowering in autumn
- **Pruning:** light pruning at the end of winter

Yellow roses

'Buff Beauty'
Moschata Hybrid. Bentall 1939

'Leverkusen'
Modern Hybrid. Kordes 1954

Description: The heavily perfumed clusters of pale apricot/buff-yellow flowers that fade to ivory as they die off, give this Shrub Rose a real grace and make it a popular choice for gardens. It also has good resistance to disease.

Position: Thanks to its supple form and spreading habit, 'Buff Beauty' is well suited to informal areas. It is versatile, being useful for hedging, but also makes a good display planted alone, grown in a container or as a small Climber against a wall, its only real requirement being enough breathing space to allow it to bloom in comfort.

Description: A robust climber, 'Leverkusen' flowers generously, producing pale yellow, semi-double blooms that give off a delicate lemon fragrance. As well as having an abundance of flowers, this rose has attractive, pale green foliage that offers excellent resistance to disease. It produces a particularly good display in autumn.

Position: With the refreshing, bright colour of its flowers, this rose looks highly decorative growing against many different kinds of support – a trellis, a pergola or a wall... It can also be staked and trained into a bush.

Characteristics

- **Height:** 150cm (5ft)
- **Spread:** 150cm (5ft)
- **Flowering:** continuous flowering from summer into autumn
- **Pruning:** at the end of winter

Characteristics

- **Height:** 300cm (10ft)
- **Spread:** 250cm (8ft 6in)
- **Flowering:** repeat flowering
- **Pruning:** normal pruning at the end of winter

'Korresia'
Floribunda. Kordes 1973

'Graham Thomas'
David Austin 1983

Description: The Kordes nametag usually denotes a reliable rose that will be extremely healthy. This variety of Bush Rose, also known as 'Friesia', produces excellent, fully double blooms of a pure, bright yellow. Carried on a compact bush, these highly scented roses are set off to perfection by their gleaming, light green leaves.

Position: This plain and simple rose can be used to good effect in beds and borders. It also makes an ideal flower for cutting – its perfect shape and glowing colour look at their best when part of a bouquet.

Description: David Austin, who created this delightful upright Shrub Rose, has carried off a number of prizes for it. Deep yellow double flowers with a fragrance reminiscent of violets, are set off beautifully by dense, dark green foliage. The flowering season lasts from early summer to late autumn.

Position: A group of three 'Graham Thomas' planted together in the centre of a bed or border, make a splendid show. Alternatively, one rose can be trained as a small Climber, growing up a pillar or some other form of support.

Characteristics

- **Height:** 75cm (30in)
- **Spread:** 60cm (2ft)
- **Flowering:** repeat flowering
- **Pruning:** normal pruning at the end of winter

Characteristics

- **Height:** 120cm (4ft)
- **Spread:** 120cm (4ft)
- **Flowering:** repeat flowering
- **Pruning:** at the end of winter

Yellow roses

'Peace'
Hybrid Tea. Meilland 1945

'Golden Wings'
Modern Hybrid. Shepherd 1953

Description: Probably one of the best-known varieties in the world, this Bush Rose has extremely large flowers ranging from pale to dark yellow and edged in pink, or even red, according to the soil type and the local climate. Also known as 'Mme A. Meilland', this rose was given to each of the 49 delegates who met in San Francisco in 1945 for the formation of the United Nations. Since that time, its popularity has never waned, which is hardly surprising, because, in addition to its lovely flowers, it has robustly healthy, glossy foliage as well as a subtle fragrance.

Position: Good in beds and borders or in low hedging, although it needs room to breathe and space to grow.

Characteristics

- **Height:** 100cm (39in) (also available as a Climber, growing to 300cm/9ft 9in)
- **Spread:**: 90cm (36in)
- **Flowering:** repeat flowering
- **Pruning:** normal pruning at the end of winter

Description: A beautiful and highly popular Shrub Rose with sulphur-yellow single flowers with prominent ochre-tinted stamens at their centre. 'Golden Wings' flowers freely from June onwards and also has a gentle, very pleasant perfume. It has an upright habit and light green foliage that has good resistance to disease.

Position: Whether grown alone, or with several other 'Golden Wings', this rose is shown to good effect. It looks superb in a hedge if positioned alongside shrubs such as elder (e.g. *Sambucus racemosa* 'Plumosa Aurea' or European red elder) that have golden foliage.

Characteristics

- **Height:** 120cm (4ft)
- **Spread:** 120cm (4ft)
- **Flowering:** repeat flowering
- **Pruning:** cut back the branches by about one-third at the end of winter

Rosa banksiae 'Lutea'
China. Introduced into Europe in 1824

'Gloire de Dijon'
Tea. Jacotot 1853

Description: A rather delicate rose that requires a sheltered position with plenty of sun as it is likely to be susceptible to frost. Once established, however, it produces beautiful cascades of pale yellow double flowers. Still grown in its natural state in China, for anyone who loves wild roses, it is a sheer delight. Arched in habit, its long branches are almost completely devoid of thorns. It normally finishes flowering by early summer.

Position: This Climber grows vigorously and needs strong support in a sheltered location, away from any sharp variations in temperature.

Description: This is a popular choice and a long-established fixture in many mature gardens thanks to its large, round, quartered flowers of a buff-yellow colour, with tones of beige and orange. This Climber flowers freely, with a fragrant perfume, from early summer through to autumn. A disadvantage is that it is vulnerable to black spot and to losing its lower leaves. However, both problems can be tackled easily by preventative spraying with a fungicide and planting a clematis at its base.

Position: This rose normally works particularly well trained against a wall, or on a trellis or a pergola.

Characteristics

- **Height:** 600cm (20ft)
- **Spread:** 300cm (10ft)
- **Flowering:** single flowering
- **Pruning:** simply remove any dead wood after flowering

Characteristics

- **Height:** 350cm (11ft 6in)
- **Spread:** 250cm (8ft 6in)
- **Flowering:** repeat flowering
- **Pruning:** normal pruning at the end of winter

Field roses

This chapter is devoted to the more natural-looking field roses, which are just as happy rambling through a hedge as growing in a bed or border in a country garden. Rather than pick out those that are single or repeat flowering, I have concentrated on the charm of their appearance.

Shrub roses

'Marguerite Hilling'
Moyesii Hybrid. Hilling 1959

'Archiduc Joseph'
Tea. Nabonnand 1872

Description: Also known as 'Pink Nevada', this is a sport (mutation) of the 'Nevada' rose, which it resembles in every respect except for the colour of the flowers, which are not white but a pretty, intense shade of pink. It flowers in June and September.

Both 'Marguerite Hilling' and 'Nevada' will tolerate poor soil and have no real need to be pruned, making them particularly suitable for inexperienced gardeners who have space to fill but only a limited amount of time.

Position: Like the 'Nevada', this rose can be grown on its own, as part of a hedge or beneath trees, providing it has enough room.

Description: Tea Roses are often thought of as delicate, but in fact they are often extremely hardy and remarkably vigorous. The blooms of 'Archiduc Joseph' are fully double, with mainly pink petals, which take on shades of peach, purple or orange according to the amount of exposure in their position and the type and quality of the soil. Its perfume is long-lasting and unvarying in its delicacy, while the dark, glossy foliage is produced on branches that are almost devoid of thorns.

Position: A relatively small-sized shrub, this rose is suitable for use in beds or in borders.

Characteristics

- **Height:** 250cm (8ft 9in)
- **Spread:** 200cm (6ft 6in)
- **Flowering:** repeat flowering
- **Pruning:** this rose needs no pruning – cut out any dead wood as necessary

Characteristics

- **Height:** 120cm (4ft)
- **Spread:** 100cm (39in)
- **Flowering:** repeat flowering
- **Pruning:** light pruning at the end of winter – pruning too hard will result in reduced flowering

'Alchemist'
Modern Hybrid. Kordes 1956

'Joséphine de Beauharnais'
Repeat flowering Hybrid. Guillot Fils 1865

Description: Primarily a Climber, this rose can also be trained as a Shrub Rose. The large, fully double flowers, which are a beautiful shade of orangey-yellow and give off an intoxicating perfume, lend it the appearance of an Old Rose. Unfortunately, this variety has become rather rare, so it's high time to reverse this tendency. It has olive-green foliage that provides a perfect complement for the apricot tinges of its flowers, although these disappear quite early on in the season. Disease resistance is good.

Position: This delightful rose can be grown singly, but also does well trained against a wall, or on an arch or column.

Description: The Empress Josephine, Napoleon's wife, had a passion for roses, and this one, her namesake, pays her tremendous homage. Its large, double flowers are of an extremely delicate, silvery-pink hue, opening out into a lovely round shape and giving a glimpse of a delightful greenish centre. The supple branches are covered in fine prickles, and bear light green foliage that remains healthy.

Position: The fresh beauty of this rose makes it an ideal mainstay for landscaped hedging. It works well mixed with roses that are white or a deep shade of red, but looks equally spectacular if grown by itself.

Characteristics
- ■ **Height:** 350cm (12ft)
- ■ **Spread:** 250cm (8ft 9in)
- ■ **Flowering:** single flowering
- ■ **Pruning:** after flowering

Characteristics
- ■ **Height:** 200cm (6ft 6in)
- ■ **Spread:** 120cm (4ft)
- ■ **Flowering:** single flowering
- ■ **Pruning:** light pruning after flowering

Shrub roses

'Sourire d'Orchidée'
Croix 1985

'Pleine de Grâce'
Lens 1983

Description: Few will remain immune to the charms of this lovely rose, with its large clusters of single flowers with a pearly pink hue that turns to white before the petals drop. The rosebuds are a delicious candy-pink adding a contrasting splash of colour to the glossy, robust foliage.

Position: This is a generous, supple shrub, ideal for planting in a solo position, since it benefits from repeat flowering throughout the summer. It can also be encouraged to climb, when it can reach a height of around 400cm (13ft).

Description: Although often used as a Climber, this rose is even more spectacular when grown as a shrub. Its long, arching branches reaching up to 200cm (6ft 6in), become covered with a multitude of single, pure white flowers centred around long yellow stamens. Heavily perfumed, these flowers stand out against a glossy, yellowish-green foliage. This is a single-flowering rose that blooms in early summer, its flowers dieing off to leave gorgeous, full globe-like hips.

Position: 'Pleine de Grâce' can be used in a solo position or in a wild hedge or mixed bed, as well as being trained to climb up a tree or a pergola.

Characteristics

- **Height:** 180cm (6ft) when kept as a shrub
- **Spread:** 150cm (5ft)
- **Flowering:** repeat flowering
- **Pruning:** normal pruning at the end of winter

Characteristics

- **Height:** 250cm (8ft 9in) or 400–600cm (13–18ft) if used as a Climber)
- **Spread:** 400cm (13ft)
- **Flowering:** single flowering
- **Pruning:** pruning is not needed – simply cut out the dead wood as necessary

'Nevada'
Moyesii Hybrid. Dot 1927

'Cerise Bouquet'
Multibracteata Hybrid. Kordes 1958

Description: It would be difficult to find a more forgiving, less demanding rose than the 'Nevada'. This vigorous shrub grows long, arching branches that gradually reach down to the soil. They are a handsome, reddish-brown and bear dense foliage but have almost no thorns. The large flowers are a white tinged with yellow and give off a light, attractive perfume. They bloom in profusion, periodically throughout the summer, with an abundant display in the autumn.

Position: Whether grown singly, in a hedge or under light tree cover which, unlike many roses, it will tolerate, 'Nevada' will be perfectly at home as long as it has plenty of room in which to grow.

Description: Every garden should have at least one example of this no-nonsense rose. But make sure the garden is large, as this extremely vigorous shrub can easily reach a height and spread of 350cm (12ft). Positively laden with flowers, the arching, spiky, branches with their dense, dark green foliage make a wonderful spectacle. The blooms are semi-double, cerise in colour, and give off a delicious scent of raspberries. Its abundance of beautiful blooms more than makes up for its single flowering.

Position: Perfect either by itself or in a mixed border, this rose can also be trained as a Climber and grown in light shade.

Characteristics

■ **Height:** 250cm (8ft 9in)
■ **Spread:** 200cm (6ft 6in)
■ **Flowering:** repeat flowering
■ **Pruning:** this rose should not be pruned – simply cut out any dead wood

Characteristics

■ **Height:** 350cm (12ft)
■ **Spread:** 350cm (12ft)
■ **Flowering:** single flowering
■ **Pruning:** needs only a little light pruning after flowering

Shrub roses

'Felicia'
Moschata Hybrid. Pemberton 1928

'Salet'
Centifolia Muscosa. Lacharme 1854

Description: A revival of interest in Old Roses has led to the rediscovery of this very handsome Shrub Rose. A pretty pink colour, with a dash of salmon, its medium-sized, double blooms hang in clusters, flowering throughout the summer and giving off a delicious musky fragrance. The foliage is a healthy, dark green, which sets off the fresh beauty of the petals to perfection.

Position: Extremely decorative in a solo position on a lawn, this rose can also be used for hedging. Its blooms are perfect for cutting.

Description: A reliable Moss Rose, 'Salet' has delighted many a lover of Old Roses thanks to its continuous flowering from spring through to autumn. Its large, pure pink blooms tend to darken at the end of the season and have an attractive heaviness. The flowers are so heavily fragrant that this rose could just as easily have been featured in the section devoted to perfumed roses. This is a loose-structured shrub with light green foliage.

Position: Magnificent in a mixed border, this rose looks good in the company of a graceful perennial such as scabious or the delicate, gentle colours of aquilegia. It is also ideal for growing in a container.

Characteristics

- **Height:** 150cm (5ft)
- **Spread:** 120cm (4ft)
- **Flowering:** repeat flowering
- **Pruning:** prune at the end of the winter – lightly to encourage the shrub to increase in size, or hard to keep it small

Characteristics

- **Height:** 120cm (4ft)
- **Spread:** 100cm (39in)
- **Flowering:** repeat flowering
- **Pruning:** normal pruning at the end of winter

'Ballerina'
Moschata Hybrid. Bentall 1937

'Heritage'
David Austin 1984

Description: A charming rose with all the freshness of a spring morning, 'Ballerina' has an upright stance, its branches topped by large clusters of pink, single flowers that fade to almost white in the centre. This is a reliable rose that can adapt itself to a number of locations, with lightly perfumed blooms that are slightly reminiscent of hydrangeas. Small, orange hips appear in the autumn, displayed against gleaming, healthy foliage.

Position: 'Ballerina' lends itself to a number of possible uses and can be grown equally well in a container. It has a good structure and is tolerant of shade.

Description: Here is another English rose with an international reputation. Its medium-sized, cup-shaped flowers are bright pink in the centre, with the outer petals becoming progressively paler. Their perfume has fruity notes combining the fragrance of carnations, honey and myrrh. Extremely robust, this bushy shrub has healthy foliage that is rarely susceptible to disease.

Position: Create a superb effect by planting several of these roses together – in groups of three or five in the centre of a mixed border. Alternatively, try growing them underneath a lilac tree with a cluster of peonies nearby.

Characteristics

- ■ **Height:** 120cm (4ft)
- ■ **Spread:** 120cm (4ft)
- ■ **Flowering:** repeat flowering
- ■ **Pruning:** prune at the end of winter

Characteristics

- ■ **Height:** 120cm (4ft)
- ■ **Spread:** 120cm (4ft)
- ■ **Flowering:** repeat flowering
- ■ **Pruning:** cut back by about one-third at the end of winter

Climbing Roses

'New Dawn'
Wichuraiana Hybrid. Somerset Nursery 1930

'Pierre de Ronsard'
Meiviolin. Meilland 1986

Description: A perfect rose and, in addition, an undemanding one, 'New Dawn' has double flowers of an elegant, pearly pink hue. It has pretty, rounded buds, opening out against abundant foliage that is a vivid dark green. The perfume is light, but noticeable nevertheless. This rose has one main advantage over the others in the same family – its long flowering season, which lasts right through into autumn.

Position: Happy when given a wall, a pergola or a fence to climb over, this rose can tolerate a north-facing position.

Description: Similar to the Old Roses but more robust, just as many Hybrid Teas, the globe-shaped blooms of 'Pierre de Ronsard' are a delicate pink bordering on white. Some catalogues describe them as 'fragrant', although others disagree. Often grown as a Climber, 'Pierre de Ronsard' can also be grown as a vigorous bush. It has healthy, glossy foliage, but any signs of black spot should be treated without delay.

Position: Best grown against a wall or fence, this rose can also be grown on its own if you decide to train it as a shrub.

Characteristics

- **Height:** 500cm (17ft 6in)
- **Spread:** 300cm (9ft 9in)
- **Flowering:** repeat flowering
- **Pruning:** normal pruning at the end of winter

Characteristics

- **Height:** 250cm (8ft 9in)
- **Spread:** 150cm (5ft)
- **Flowering:** repeat flowering
- **Pruning:** normal pruning at the end of winter

'Ghislaine de Féligonde'
Multiflora Hybrid. Turbat 1916

'Aimée Vibert'
Noisettiana. Vibert 1828

Description: This magnificent rose deserves to be more widely grown. Its elegant and fragrant flowers open out in clusters of apricot pink that turns to yellow and then to cream. It flowers continuously and has healthy, attractively glossy foliage and stems that are almost free of thorns. As with any rose that produces such an array of colours, it is advisable to plant it in a slightly shaded position in order to maintain the intensity of the colours.

Position: Allowed to grow against an old wall or over an arch, this rose won't disappoint. Grown as a shrub, it will blend into a hedge or can be planted on its own.

Description: Not surprisingly, this is also known as 'Bouquet de la mariée' or 'bride's bouquet'. It has an exquisite freshness, with clusters of pure white pompons borne on sturdy stems that are almost thornless. The fresh and delicate buds are plump and rounded, with a pretty perfume once they open. Magnificent foliage and a long flowering season are two of this rose's other good points.

Position: Happy growing over an arch or a pillar, or against a wall, this rose can also be trained as a shrub.

Characteristics
- **Height:** 250cm (8ft 9in)
- **Spread:** 250cm (8ft 9in)
- **Flowering:** heavy repeat flowering
- **Pruning:** normal pruning at the end of winter

Characteristics
- **Height:** 350cm (12ft)
- **Spread:** 300cm (10ft)
- **Flowering:** repeat flowering
- **Pruning:** normal pruning at the end of winter

Climbing Roses

'Clair Matin'
Meilland 1960

'Laure Davoust'
Multiflora Hybrid. Laffay 1834

Description: Clusters of semi-double flowers of a bright pink mixed with ivory are carried on supple branches of a handsome chocolate-brown. 'Clair Matin's' coral-pink buds contrast beautifully with the delicacy of the petals. After flowering abundantly in June, the blooms come and go during the summer months, returning in profusion in September. The perfume is pretty, with a fragrance of wild roses.

Position: Given the right support, this little Climber can reach a height of about 300cm (10ft), making it ideal for growing up a pillar, a low wall or over a small arch. It will look equally good as part of a hedge or standing alone in a lawn.

Description: When a rose that has been around for as long as this one can still be seen embellishing many gardens, it must be because it has all the qualities needed to see off the competition. And the competition is rather fierce! Still, there is no way that anyone could fail to be delighted by its bright pink, quartered blooms, which open out into lovely, romantic bouquets.

Position: This is a no-nonsense Climber that will quickly take full possession of any sturdy support in a sunny position. Adding a late-flowering clematis solves the problem of this being a single flowering rose.

Characteristics

- **Height:** 250cm (8ft 9in)
- **Spread:** 120cm (4ft)
- **Flowering:** repeat flowering
- **Pruning:** at the end of winter, cut back any secondary branches to three buds

Characteristics

- **Height:** 500cm (17ft 6in)
- **Spread:** 250cm (8ft 9in)
- **Flowering:** single flowering
- **Pruning:** simply remove any dead wood

'Albertine'
Luciae Hybrid. Barbier 1900

'Paul Transon'
Wichuraiana Hybrid. Barbier 1900

Description: If you are looking for a beautiful, richly-coloured rose with lots of fragrance, then this is the rose for you! If you like its vermilion-coloured buds, you will be delighted by its blooms, with their shades of copper and salmon that change to a bright pink. The heavy fragrance is no less attention-seizing. Perfect as a Climber, this rose can also be trained as a shrub; in either case, a semi-shaded position will suit it best. Its branches have an abundance of foliage and are very prickly. Beware of a tendency to powdery mildew.

Position: This extremely vigorous rose will need solid supports to take its weight.

Description: A rose with an exquisite fragrance of apples and a very handsome colour. Its double flowers open out in small clusters that are an elegant, bright, salmon-pink, streaked with luminous coppery-orange. The foliage is vigorous and healthy, with very glossy, light green leaves.

Position: The warm colour tones of 'Paul Transon' will look resplendent planted near a yellow rose such as 'Golden Showers'. Like this rose, it can tolerate a semi-shaded position.

Characteristics

- **Height:** 650cm (22ft)
- **Spread:** 350cm (12ft)
- **Flowering:** single flowering, but with a fairly long flowering season
- **Pruning:** just after flowering

Characteristics

- **Height:** 300cm (10ft)
- **Spread:** 250cm (8ft 9in)
- **Flowering:** repeat flowering
- **Pruning:** normal pruning at the end of winter

Climbing Roses

'Crimson Glory'
Hybrid Tea. Jackson and Perkins 1946

'Bleu Magenta'
Multiflora Hybrid. Van Houtte 1900

Description: This is a rose that brings memories flooding back for me since it used to grow at the front of my childhood home. Its large, dark red flowers with a purple tinge seem to have been cut from a piece of velvet. A vigorous Climber with lush foliage, it is best if trained on a sturdy support. And if my memory serves me well, its deep, strong perfume is like a blend of jasmine and lemon. A truly exceptional repeat flowering rose!

Position: This Climber needs support when grown against walls, pergolas or trellis.

Description: Displayed against elegant, dark foliage that covers stems that are almost smooth, the highly delicate flowers of 'Bleu Magenta' bloom in deep purple clusters. Prettily folded over at the centre, its petals make a gentle corolla around pronounced yellow stamens. Although not repeat flowering, it blooms for a long time in the summer.

Position: A Rambler with thick foliage, this rose is ideal for providing quick-growing cover on an extremely wide range of different supports, providing they are strong enough to take the weight. It is worth noting that this rose quite likes a semi-shaded position.

Characteristics

- **Height:** 400cm (13ft)
- **Spread:** 250cm (8ft 9in)
- **Flowering:** repeat flowering
- **Pruning:** normal pruning at the end of winter

Characteristics

- **Height:** 400cm (13ft)
- **Spread:** 350cm (12ft)
- **Flowering:** single flowering
- **Pruning:** optional

'Grand-mère Jenny'
Hybrid Tea. Meilland 1958

'Easley's Golden Rambler'
Wichuraiana Hybrid. Easley 1932

Description: If you are starting to wonder why so far in this section, there has been distinct tendency towards the colour pink, this rose will begin to redress the balance. Its flowers are a primrose-yellow with shades of apricot and rather indistinct stripes of pink. The blooms are an impressive size, with no less than thirty petals and flower freely. The foliage is healthy and the stems grow vigorously. The perfect rose to bring an original splash of colour to the garden and fairly resistant to disease.

Position: 'Grand-mère Jenny' is a good rose for growing against walls and pillars.

Description: This is one of the best yellow Climbers. Borne on vigorous stems that are bristling with highly decorative reddish thorns, the double flowers are brightly coloured, with a tousled appearance and an attractive perfume. The foliage is glossy, and offers complete resistance to disease.

Position: Even poor soil and a shaded position will not thwart this lovely rose. When positioned against a tree, its branches hang in beautiful, luminous cascades.

Characteristics

- **Height:** 500cm (17ft 6in)
- **Spread:** 300cm (10ft)
- **Flowering:** repeat flowering
- **Pruning:** normal pruning at the end of winter

Characteristics

- **Height:** 500cm (17ft 6in)
- **Spread:** 450cm (15ft)
- **Flowering:** single flowering
- **Pruning:** simply remove any dead wood

Rambling Roses

'Neige d'Avril'
Multiflora Hybrid. Robichon 1908

'American Pillar'
Wichuraiana Hybrid. Van Fleet 1902

Description: 'Neige d'Avril', meaning 'april snow', conjures up a rose with a lovely, fresh quality, like an orchard at apple-blossom time. This is a very early-flowering rose, which often takes the lead over other plants in the garden. The semi-double flowers come into bloom in late April to early May, their virginal whiteness attracting attention for at least three weeks. The blooms exude a bright, apple fragrance and in autumn give way to small, orangey-red fruits. This rose has splendid, healthy foliage that stays disease-free.

Position: Make the most of its early flowering and combine this rose with other, later-flowering varieties that will take over when 'Neige d'Avril' starts to fade.

Description: The vigour of this rose is legendary. Its large bouquets of carmine-red single flowers with a white centre are still a popular feature in today's gardens, along with the unavoidable 'Queen Elizabeth' (which I had to restrain myself from including in this collection).

Position: 'American Pillar' makes short work of rambling over frames and supports of all kinds, with its thick, spiny stems and glossy foliage. Even in poor soil it performs extremely well.

Characteristics

- **Height:** 600cm (20ft)
- **Spread:** 400cm (13ft)
- **Flowering:** single flowering
- **Pruning:** not necessary

Characteristics

- **Height:** 500cm (17ft 6in)
- **Spread:** 400cm (13ft)
- **Flowering:** single flowering, in June
- **Pruning:** after flowering

'Bobbie James'
Multiflora Hybrid. Sunningdale 1961

'Mermaid'
Bracteata Hybrid. Paul 1919

Description: A rose with great vigour that can send out sturdy, thorny branches to scale the tallest of trees. In summer, dazzling bouquets of its semi-double, fragrant white flowers open out in abundant masses and the light-coloured foliage is luxuriant and robust.

Position: The prodigious size of this rose demands that it has room to breath and that it is used only on very solid supports. An old fruit tree is ideal, providing that it is large enough and there is no danger of the trunk being decayed. You might equally decide to let this Rambler run through some hedging, which will quickly become an impenetrable, dense mass.

Characteristics

- **Height:** 900cm (30ft)
- **Spread:** 600cm (20ft)
- **Flowering:** single flowering
- **Pruning:** none necessary

Description: If your preference is normally for roses with double blooms, it's still worth taking a look at this Climber. Although its blooms are single, its large flowers have the elegant simplicity of wild roses, with primrose-yellow petals encircling golden stamens. It flowers profusely throughout the summer until the first frosts. Its dark brown stems are extremely thorny, but combined with the lush, dark green foliage, make a magnificent backdrop for the flowers.

Position: A little more fragile than other roses, 'Mermaid' can fall victim to frost and needs a sunny position either against a sheltered wall or in a generally mild climate, in order to establish itself. Although it is slow to grow, this rose is one of the most beautiful of its type, and is well worth the wait.

Characteristics

- **Height:** 750cm (23ft)
- **Spread:** 500cm (17ft 6in)
- **Flowering:** repeat flowering
- **Pruning:** none necessary

Rambling Roses

'Toby Tristram'
Multiflora Hybrid

'Sir Cedric Morris'
Rosa glauca. Morris 1979

Description: This is a Rambler that is often recommended by rose-growers. It produces splendid bouquets of single, creamy-coloured flowers, often with as many as 50 blooms opening out on one stem. The foliage is mid-green in colour, abundant and compact. And, as if all this were not enough, a profusion of small hips appear in the autumn, making a visual treat for the eyes as well as a fine feast for the birds.

Position: Any sound support will suit this rose, and the renewed interest created by its hips in autumn, merit it a prominent position in the garden. An old rose bush with a mixture of perennials and shrubs bearing blue or pink flowers growing at its base would complement it perfectly.

Characteristics

- **Height:** 800cm (26ft)
- **Spread:** 500cm (16ft 6in)
- **Flowering:** single flowering
- **Pruning:** needs no pruning

Description: Discovered among some *Rosa glauca* seedlings by Sir Cedric Morris, this Rambler is endowed, like its parent, with handsome, blue-green, purplish foliage, although this is less pronounced than that of its parent. The flowers bloom in large clusters of prettily-perfumed, regularly-spaced white flowers. Although flowering occurs just once in the summer, it paves the way for an array of small, round hips, almost orange in colour, which look very decorative in autumn.

Position: 'Sir Cedric Morris' is held in great affection by rose-lovers. It is a vigorous grower and as with all Climbers that reach a great size, it needs a strong support. It is best suited to a natural setting and will tolerate shade.

Characteristics

- **Height:** 900cm (30ft)
- **Spread:** 600cm (20ft)
- **Flowering:** single flowering
- **Pruning:** needs no pruning

'Paul's Himalayan Musk'
Moschata Hybrid. Paul 1916

'Seagull'
Multiflora Hybrid. Pritchard 1907

Description: This extremely vigorous rose is one that I couldn't possibly do without in my garden. It is single flowering, but always makes a spectacular display. Grouped together in loose clusters and with a gently drooping appearance that adds to their charm, the rosette-shaped flowers are a lilac-pink with flashes of white. Nicely perfumed, they open out in the midst of dark green foliage with bronze tints. The branches are very supple, attaching themselves with ease to their support, such as a tree, with their sharp thorns.

Position: A useful rose for concealing an untidy bit of the garden, or a dead tree or unkempt hedge... or just to grow up a simple pergola. Whatever support you choose, make sure that it is solid.

Characteristics

- **Height:** 700cm (24ft)
- **Spread:** 350cm (12ft)
- **Flowering:** single flowering
- **Pruning:** none necessary

Description: This is a highly-perfumed and vigorous Rambler that opens up in clusters of small, white, single flowers with golden stamens at the centre. Although it does not repeat flower, 'Seagull' does have a long flowering season, and visual interest is renewed in the autumn, when it becomes covered with a multitude of small, shiny red hips.

Position: There are many situations suitable for this rose. A tree will provide an ideal natural support for its vigorous branches, but a tall wall, even a north-facing one, will be transformed when it comes into bloom, and again in autumn when the hips arrive. It can tolerate poor soil conditions.

Characteristics

- **Height:** 750cm (25ft)
- **Spread:** 450cm (13ft 3in)
- **Flowering:** single flowering
- **Pruning:** needs no pruning

Single flowering roses

'Fantin-Latour'
Centifolia

'Variegata di Bologna'
Bourbon. Bonfiglioli 1909

Description: A gorgeous rose with fully double blooms of deep pink that grow in clusters, opening out into a paler, flesh-pink, that contrasts beautifully with the glossy foliage. When fully open the flowers are flattish, revealing a glimpse of green at their centre. Flowering in June, the perfume is delicate and sweet.

Position: The well-balanced shape of this rose means that it looks equally good in the middle of a lawn or in a mixed border.

Description: Flesh-pink in colour and streaked with crimson, the flowers of this Italian rose have a great freshness. The blooms are open-cupped and fully double, giving off a heady, heavy perfume.

Position: Usually grown as a Shrub, this rose can equally well be trained as a Climber. A sheltered position is preferable, with plenty of sunlight, although it will tolerate poorer soil.

Characteristics

- **Height:** 150cm (5ft)
- **Spread:** 120cm (4ft)
- **Flowering:** single flowering
- **Pruning:** after flowering – be sure to keep the overall shape

Characteristics

- **Height:** 180cm (6ft)
- **Spread:** 150cm (5ft)
- **Flowering:** this rose is single flowering, although a few flowers may repeat in the autumn
- **Pruning:** at the end of winter

'Constance Spry'
Modern Hybrid. Austin 1961

'Fritz Nobis'
Modern Hybrid. Kordes 1940

Description: Another truly lovely rose, and one with more than a passing resemblance to the luxuriant peony. 'Constance Spry' can be forgiven for not being repeat flowering thanks to its profusion of perfectly-shaped velvety pink petals and an unforgettable fragrance of myrrh. It flowers in abundance in June.

Position: 'Constance Spry' can be grown as a bush or trained as a Climber on a frame or against a wall. It is also worth noting that it can tolerate a semi-shaded position as well as being quite happy in water-retentive soil.

Description: This is a beautiful, dense Shrub Rose that becomes smothered with flowers in early summer. The pretty buds develop into large, double blooms that seem to waver between flesh-pink and salmon in hue. Both buds and flowers give off a clove-like fragrance. In the autumn, the branches become swathed in a profusion of small, shiny orange hips.

Position: This rose looks splendid at the back of a bed. Fill in the period between summer flowers and autumn fruit by planting a clematis to grow through its branches and flower in between times.

Characteristics

- **Height:** 200cm (6ft 6in)
- **Spread:** 150cm (5ft)
- **Flowering:** single flowering
- **Pruning:** after flowering

Characteristics

- **Height:** 150cm (5ft)
- **Spread:** 120cm (4ft)
- **Flowering:** single flowering
- **Pruning:** light pruning after flowering

Single flowering roses

'Madame Hardy'
Damascena. Hardy 1832

'Louis van Tyle'
Gallica. Before 1846

Description: It would be difficult to find a more striking white than in the flowers of this lovely Damask Rose. Its fully double blooms have petals that curve out prettily to reveal a glimpse of a greenish centre, and give off a noticeable and powerful fragrance with a hint of lemon. The flowers are set off by vigorous foliage with attractive leaves that are yellow-tinged even when young.

Position: A beautiful shrub that can be planted equally well by itself, or in a bed among perennials and flowering shrubs. Dress up the space beneath it by planting pink geraniums or a clump of delicate *Gaura lindheimerii* (bee blossom).

Description: These beautiful double roses are difficult to resist. Their blooms open out into quarters, with mauve-pink centres encircled by an outer layer of pinkish-white petals. The flowers have a very unusual colouring and the added luxury of an exquisite, opulent perfume.

Position: This medium-sized shrub can be used for hedging and will also bring a touch of originality to beds and borders. In order not to overshadow its neighbours, make sure you choose flowers that are equally impressive, such as delphiniums or lilies, to grow nearby.

Characteristics

- **Height:** 150cm (5ft)
- **Spread:** 150cm (5ft)
- **Flowering:** single flowering
- **Pruning:** after flowering

Characteristics

- **Height:** 130cm (4ft 4in)
- **Spread:** 120cm (4ft)
- **Flowering:** single flowering
- **Pruning:** just after flowering

'Königin von Dänemark'
Alba. Booth 1826

'Jenny Duval'
Gallica. 1821

Description: Also known as 'Queen of Denmark', this vigorous shrub with grey-green foliage and thorny branches has imposing, fully double blooms that open out into quarters and are a lovely carmine in colour. The flowers produce a powerful and sweet perfume.

Position: This Shrub Rose deserves a prime position in a bed or border. For a really spectacular display, try planting some mauve delphiniums close by.

Description: On close examination the flowers of this rose reveal a surprising array of colours, with traces of mauve, a purplish brown and a flaming shade of cerise. The colours can even vary in shade according to the weather and, just at the point of fading, take on a bluish tone. The stems grow vigorously but are supple. This rose will appeal to anyone with an eye for the slightly unusual, at least in terms of colour.

Position: 'Jenny Duval' can be useful for planting along a drive or walkway, or in front of a bank of yew hedging. It will also tolerate being grown in a container.

Characteristics

- **Height:** 150cm (5ft)
- **Spread:** 120cm (4ft)
- **Flowering:** single flowering
- **Pruning:** after flowering

Characteristics

- **Height:** 120cm (4ft)
- **Spread:** 80cm (32in)
- **Flowering:** single flowering
- **Pruning:** prune just after flowering by shortening the side branches

Hedging roses

Rosa spinosissima 'Altaica'
Wild Rose Hybrid. 1820

'Lady Penzance'
Rubiginosa Hybrid. Penzance 1894

Description: This hybrid has all the characteristics of the main species, which can be found growing wild in many parts of Europe, particularly on sandy soil where they can sucker freely. The light green foliage of this rose, reminiscent of certain types of fern, is set off nicely by the dark brown stems. It blooms early, although only briefly, from May to early June, but its single, creamy-white flowers are large and attractive. They give way to purple-black hips that are highly ornamental.

Position: Its thorny branches make this an ideal rose for protective hedging. It will also tolerate light shade and poor soil.

Description: The unusual colour of this rose alone makes it worthy of interest. With single flowers of a coppery-salmon hue, a pink centre and highly visible yellow stamens, the overall effect is very appealing. Another special feature is its dark green, dentate foliage that gives off an apple-scented perfume that is particularly noticeable after rain.

Position: The supple stance of this fine shrub makes it an ideal rose for use as protective hedging. In addition, it looks superb alongside purple-leaved shrubs such as hazel or *cotinus*.

Characteristics

- **Height:** 120cm (4ft)
- **Spread:** 100cm (39in)
- **Flowering:** single flowering
- **Pruning:** the removal of any dead wood from time to time is all that is needed

Characteristics

- **Height:** 180cm (6ft)
- **Spread:** 180cm (6ft)
- **Flowering:** single flowering
- **Pruning:** not necessary

'Stanwell Perpetual'
Spinosissima Hybrid. Lee 1838

'Goldbusch'
Kordes 1954

Description: These extremely graceful double flowers of a soft, pale pink, bloom in abundance in June and repeat flower until the autumn, a quality that is rare in a botanical species. The gentle perfume of the flowers has an air of opulence. Overall, the bush has a dense appearance and the arching stems are thickly covered in thorns. The dentate leaves are an attractive green with tinges of grey.

Position: A good choice for making a moderate-sized hedge, 'Stanwell Perpetual' can also be used in conjunction with taller Shrub Roses. Planted as a front row, they will help create a thick hedge that will be twice as protective.

Description: Another Shrub Rose that is seen surprisingly rarely. Its semi-double flowers, which are pale yellow with a hint of orange, have an exquisite freshness. They give off a delicious perfume and are carried on supple branches covered in an abundance of fragrant and good-looking, pale green foliage.

Position: 'Goldbusch' works well in a group of three on a lawn, as part of a mixed border or in a natural hedge. It can also be trained as a small Climber and will tolerate poorer soils and light shade.

Characteristics

■ **Height:** 150cm (5ft)
■ **Spread:** 120cm (4ft)
■ **Flowering:** repeat flowering
■ **Pruning:** pruning is not necessary – simply cut back any dead wood as appropriate

Characteristics

■ **Height:** 250cm (8ft 9in)
■ **Spread:** 150cm (5ft)
■ **Flowering:** single flowering
■ **Pruning:** a simple tidy-up after flowering is all that is needed

Hedging roses

Rosa rugosa

Japan and some western regions of Asia.
Before 1799

'Rush'

Rosa multiflora. Lens 1983

Description: This is an extremely hardy rose that has even taken root in a number of seaside gardens. In its pink, white or red botanical form, it deserves to be given a good position in a garden, where its delicately perfumed flowers will lend immediate charm. Its hybrid forms, 'Hansa', 'Agnès' and 'Sarah Van Fleet' are also worth considering. The foliage is characteristically wrinkled and displayed on upright stems. It also has excellent resistance to disease and provides a plentiful array of hips in the autumn.

Position: *Rosa rugosa* is *the* hedging rose. To soften its rather stiff appearance, combine it with flowering shrubs such as *Kolwitzia amabilis* (Beauty Bush), which has a supple, graceful shape. Beware of planting in chalky soil, as it is prone to yellowing.

Characteristics

- **Height:** 150cm (5ft)
- **Spread:** 150cm (5ft)
- **Flowering:** repeat flowering
- **Pruning:** not always necessary – it will depend on the location

Description: This superb shrub has to be one of the loveliest creations of recent years. Flowering in abundance, its large, single blooms are pink with a white centre, and open out in generous clusters. New buds continue to appear throughout the season, ensuring that it flowers until the end of the autumn. A shrub with an excellent shape, it has good branch structure and a delicate, open appearance.

Position: Frequently recommended for use either in borders or by itself, this rose also makes beautiful hedging to partition off different sections of the garden.

Characteristics

- **Height:** 150cm (5ft)
- **Spread:** 120cm (4ft)
- **Flowering:** repeat flowering
- **Pruning:** at the end of winter, shorten the main branches by one-third, and cut the side shoots back to two or three buds

'Complicata'
Macrantha Hybrid

Rosa alba 'Semiplena'
Alba

Description: A rose with a misleading name as it is far from complicated, easy to grow and its demands are few. Its flat, single flowers are large – about 12cm (5in) across – and a uniform bright pink, with an almost-white centre that accentuates the large, golden stamens. Lightly perfumed, the flowers are borne on arching, thorny branches with attractive, grey-green foliage. Round, orange hips appear late in the season.

Position: 'Complicata' makes a marvellous show whether in a natural hedge, planted among other roses of the same type or with a mixture of deciduous and evergreen shrubs. It will tolerate a relatively poor soil.

Description: Some specialists think that this is one of the oldest rose cultivars, and it is known to have existed in Roman times. Its appearance is seductive, with large, flat, semi-double milky-white blooms with delicate golden stamens. The flowers have a powerful perfume and are used to make attar of roses. The overall shape of the plant is attractive, combining an upright stance with a degree of suppleness.

Position: 'Semiplena' is perfect grown in settings that are informal or even semi-wild. It looks splendid planted in quantity to make a hedge, and also looks good alongside various Gallica roses that have similar qualities.

Characteristics

- **Height:** 250cm (8ft 9in)
- **Spread:** 220cm (7ft 3in)
- **Flowering:** single flowering
- **Pruning:** cut back the side branches to two or three buds after flowering

Characteristics

- **Height:** 220cm (7ft 3in)
- **Spread:** 150cm (5ft)
- **Flowering:** single flowering
- **Pruning:** after flowering, shortening the main branches and the side stems by about one-third

Town roses

The somewhat superior reputation of these roses grants them privileged status in stylish urban gardens. With their straight backs and impeccable blooms they can be cut to decorate any room in the house. Ground-cover Roses are happy to brighten up any town garden and have the added advantage of being low maintenance and helping to suppress weeds.

Ground-cover Roses

'Kent'
Poulsen 1988

'Nozomi'
Miniature rambler. Onodera 1968

Description: Also known as 'White Cover', the elongated buds of this dense Ground-cover Rose open out into sparkling, semi-double flowers, with a splash of lemon at the centre. These flowers have a diameter of about 5cm (2in) and withstand wet weather well. In addition to having a flowering season that continues throughout the summer and into autumn, this rose also has the benefit of lush, gleaming foliage with excellent resistance to disease.

Position: 'Kent' will establish itself with ease. It looks good at the front of a flowerbed, in a border, or in front of a clipped box hedge, whose shiny foliage serves as an excellent backdrop, or even in a container.

Description: Created in Japan, this is a rose with a wide-spreading habit that, in June and July, is covered with a multitude of delightful, single, pale pink flowers that open out in small clusters. Lightly perfumed, the flowers harmonise beautifully with the delicate foliage, made up of a profusion of small, glossy, green leaves, tinged with red.

Position: The arched stems of this rose make it very suitable for planting on a low wall, over which it can tumble gracefully. 'Nozomi' is also an old favourite in rockeries.

Characteristics
- **Height:** 50cm (20in)
- **Spread:** 100cm (39in)
- **Flowering:** repeat flowering
- **Pruning:** dead-head regularly and remove any dead wood at the end of winter

Characteristics
- **Height:** 45cm (18in)
- **Spread:** 150cm (5ft)
- **Flowering:** single flowering
- **Pruning:** cut back at the end of winter to keep the branches at a low level

'Max Graf'
Rugosa Hybrid. Bowditch 1919

'Tapis Volant'
Lens 1982

Description: 'Max Graf' deserves a special mention as it is one of the most useful *Rugosa* hybrids. Exceptionally hardy, it grows happily in even the most mediocre soils, and one single plant can rapidly cover almost 300cm² (32ft²). It has thick foliage that is characteristic of the type, and single flowers of a lovely silvery-pink with paler centres, which give off a very pleasant, apple scent.

Position: Around the edge of a pond, on slopes or growing over a wall, this vigorous Ground-cover Rose will waste no time establishing itself. If planted at the front of a bank of shrubs, it will prevent weeds from taking too firm a hold.

Description: This low-growing rose's name means, most aptly, 'flying carpet'. Its branches are covered with abundant clusters of white roses with a tinge of pink that will repeat flower right through to the first frosts, followed by attractive hips. The robust, gleaming foliage adds to the attractive display formed by this frequent prize-winner.

Position: A perfect candidate for covering slopes and difficult corners, 'Tapis volant' looks good at the front of a bed, where it will form a lovely, flowering carpet requiring minimum care.

Characteristics

- **Height:** 50cm (20in)
- **Spread:** 300cm (10ft)
- **Flowering:** single flowering
- **Pruning:** not necessary

Characteristics

- **Height:** 30cm (12in)
- **Spread:** 115cm (42in)
- **Flowering:** repeat flowering
- **Pruning:** moderate pruning at the end of winter in order to keep a good shape

Ground-cover Roses

'Swany'
Meilland 1978

'Bonica'
Meilland 1986

Description: Don't be fooled by this rose's happy-go-lucky appearance – it is robust in the extreme. Unfussy about the type of soil, it has good disease resistance and produces spectacular clusters of white, fully double blooms, which are set off by abundant and lustrous dark green foliage.

Position: This rose can be used without any problems anywhere that its heavily flower-laden branches have room to spread out. It looks spectacular cascading down a slope, or on a terrace.

Description: 'Bonica' has all the charm of an Old Rose, but it flowers like the very best Modern Roses, producing clusters of elegant, semi-double flowers of a soft pink, at the ends of attractively arching stems. This small shrub is bushy in habit, with healthy, glossy foliage.

Position: Able to cover an area twice as wide as it is high, and unequalled in the ground-cover stakes, 'Bonica' is useful if planted as a low hedge, or to provide quick cover for slopes of many kinds.

Characteristics

- **Height:** 75cm (30in)
- **Spread:** 200cm (6ft 6in)
- **Flowering:** repeat flowering
- **Pruning:** cut back hard at the end of winter to ensure continuous flowering

Characteristics

- **Height:** 100cm (39in)
- **Spread:** 200cm (6ft 6in)
- **Flowering:** repeat flowering
- **Pruning:** normal pruning at the end of winter

'Francine Austin'
David Austin 1988

'Snow Ballet'
Clayworth 1977

Description: 'Francine Austin's' distinctive perfume − a mixture of Old Rose and musk − enhances the pretty clusters of small, white pompon flowers produced by this attractive shrub. Perfect as a ground-cover plant, it has healthy, shiny foliage that sets off the charming freshness of the flowers, which repeat frequently.

Position: A Ground-cover Rose with a cheerful appearance, it will brighten up a wide range of positions, from slopes and embankments to borders and flowerbeds.

Description: This charming variety has cup-shaped, double blooms of the purest white. The flowers, measuring about 5cm (2in) across, bloom continuously and have a strong perfume. The shrub is compact in shape, but is quite vigorous, with shiny, dark green foliage.

Position: 'Snow Ballet' is an excellent addition to a white garden for obvious reasons, but it is also suitable for use in a number of locations. It makes a delightful display planted to cover a slope, or set against a backdrop of dark-coloured evergreens.

Characteristics

- **Height:** 90cm (36in)
- **Spread:** 120cm (4ft)
- **Flowering:** repeat flowering
- **Pruning:** by about one-third at the end of winter

Characteristics

- **Height:** 40cm (16in)
- **Spread:** 100cm (39in)
- **Flowering:** repeat flowering
- **Pruning:** remove dead flowers to promote repeat flowering − pruning once every three years will be sufficient

Standards and Weeping Standards

'Sylvie Vartan'	'Magic Meillandecor'
Polyantha. Eve 1969	Meibourib. Meilland 1992

Description: André Eve's perfect creation has had time to prove itself. Named after the 1960s French pop star, several decades later, this rose is still bringing pleasure to many. It has excellent pink blooms that repeat flower throughout summer. They open out into lovely clusters that give off a delightful perfume. The foliage is robust, with good disease-resistance.

Position: With its compact, tidy appearance, this rose will look good in any well-kept garden. Its solid pink colour will be set off well by gypsophila, nepeta and scabious.

Description: With its exceptional resistance to disease, this rose has already acquired a good reputation as a ground-cover plant. Its lovely, magenta-pink flowers with golden yellow stamens repeat all summer long, cascading down its overhanging branches, their charm enhanced by a light fragrance of hawthorn. The dense foliage is dark green, marrying well with the pink hue of the flowers.

Position: Plant this rose in the centre of a mixed border, choosing a few purple delphiniums or something dark blue such as a clump of aconites to provide an attractive contrast.

Characteristics

- **Spread:** 60cm (24in)
- **Flowering:** repeat flowering
- **Pruning:** normal pruning at the end of winter – retain only three to five main branches

Characteristics

- **Spread:** 90cm (36in)
- **Flowering:** repeat flowering
- **Pruning:** prune at the end of winter – remove all weak stems and shorten the main branches and side shoots

'Phyllis Bide'
Polyantha Hybrid. Bide 1923

'Winchester Cathedral'
Austin 1988

Description: A natural-looking rose, 'Phyllis Bide' is made up of clusters of flowers that combine a variety of colour tints ranging from pink and yellow to cream and salmon. The healthy, abundant foliage comprises small, shiny, narrow leaves.

Position: 'Phyllis Bide' has vigorous, thorn-free branches that sweep gracefully downwards. Fill the space beneath it by planting Lady's Mantle, euphorbia, achilleas or yellow crocosmias.

Description: A sport (mutation) of 'Mary Rose', this well-known variety has taken on all the attributes of its parent. Its splendid double blooms are an immaculate white and repeat throughout the summer. They give off a gentle fragrance with notes of honey and almonds. With glossy, healthy foliage, this is an extremely elegant rose of generous proportions.

Position: Stunning in a small, city garden, this would also be perfect for inclusion in a white garden. An ideal accompaniment might be white lavender, clipped yew and hostas.

Characteristics

- **Spread:** 90cm (36in)
- **Flowering:** repeat flowering
- **Pruning:** at the end of winter, shorten the main branches and cut back the lateral branches to three or four buds

Characteristics

- **Spread:** 60cm (24in)
- **Flowering:** repeat flowering
- **Pruning:** normal pruning at the end of winter – cut back the branches to two or three buds from the grafting point

Standards and Weeping Standards

'Rustica'
Floribunda. Meilland 1981

'Auguste Gervais'
Wichuraiana Hybrid. Barbier 1918

Description: When roses with large flowers are used as Standards in town gardens, they can sometimes look rather awkward and out of place. However, 'Rustica' poses no such problem. Its large, creamy-yellow blooms pale towards the edges and have a deliciously tousled appearance. Opening out into gently drooping clusters of flowers, they contrast prettily with the elegant, matt green foliage.

Position: This Standard Rose would look stunning surrounded by Lady's Mantle and pale blue scabious.

Description: Although better known as a Climber, when it can reach a spread of 400–500cm (13–16ft), this rose also lends itself well to being grown as a Standard. Its semi-double blooms open out in copper-yellow clusters and then change prettily to ivory before withering. They repeat flower throughout the summer and give off a very pleasing perfume. The gleaming, dark green foliage is a perfect foil for the flowers.

Position: Taken from a very prolific Rambler, this Standard is so vigorous that it has no need of companion plants to bolster its display – it looks splendid when grown alone.

Characteristics

- **Spread:** 60cm (24in)
- **Flowering:** repeat flowering
- **Pruning:** cut back all the branches to two or three buds at the end of the winter – remove all shoots that have appeared along the main stem

Characteristics

- **Spread:** 90cm (36in)
- **Flowering:** single flowering, but with a long flowering period
- **Pruning:** after flowering, shorten the main branches and take the side branches back to about three buds

'Canary Bird'
Xanthina Hybrid. China 1911

'Aviateur Blériot'
Luciae Hybrid. Fauque 1910

Description: 'Canary Bird' produces long, slender branches that support fern-like leaves which contribute to the delicate appearance of this Shrub Rose, which nevertheless is a vigorous grower. Flowering early, in April or May, the single blooms are bright yellow, with projecting stamens and a musky perfume. The flowering period is very brief, although a few flowers may repeat in the autumn.

Position: Grown as a Standard, 'Canary Bird' is extremely elegant. Golden variegated sage or cream-coloured Californian poppies grown at its feet will enhance the overall effect.

Description: If you have a corner of the garden that needs brightening up, this rose, notable for its unusual colouring, will do the trick. Its lovely, orangey-yellow double flowers have a unique luminosity, opening out in clusters against dark green foliage. The perfume has a pleasant magnolia fragrance. Grafted from a Rambling Rose, this Standard has an attractive, weeping form.

Position: Place two of these roses at the end of a path, one on either side. Alternatively, grow one singly with a clump of 'Johnson Blue' geraniums planted beneath, to complete the display.

Characteristics

- **Spread:** 90cm (36in)
- **Flowering:** single flowering
- **Pruning:** light pruning after flowering

Characteristics

- **Spread:** 90cm (36in)
- **Flowering:** : single flowering
- **Pruning:** after flowering, removing any shoots on the main stem

Roses for the balcony

'Grüss an Aachen'
Floribunda. Geduldig 1909

'Madame Louis Lévêque'
Centifolia Muscosa. Lévêque 1898

Description: Quite why this rose has become less popular recently remains a total mystery. Grouped in clusters, the very full double flowers are a beautiful, creamy white with tinges of flesh pink or peach and are sweetly perfumed. Low in height, this pretty Bush Rose also has lovely, dense foliage that has excellent resistance to disease.

Position: If grown in a garden, this rose would be perfect in beds and borders. It looks every bit as good on a terrace or balcony, where it will continue to flower until the autumn.

Description: This is one of the most attractive roses suitable for use on a balcony or terrace (but not only there, of course...). It has moss-covered buds that are lovely in their own right, but once the ample, round, pale pink blooms with their silken petals appear, the glorious picture is complete. A superb rose with an upright habit, the foliage is dark green.

Position: Grow 'Madame Louis Lévêque' in a sunny position on the terrace or balcony. Surround it with nepetas or lavender and it will really turn heads.

Characteristics

- **Height:** 50cm (20in)
- **Spread:** 50cm (20in)
- **Flowering:** repeat flowering
- **Pruning:** normal pruning at the end of winter

Characteristics

- **Height:** 120cm (4ft)
- **Spread:** 100cm (39in)
- **Flowering:** light repeat flowering
- **Pruning:** cut back lightly at the end of winter

'Souvenir d'Adolphe Turc'
Polyantha. Turc 1926

'Little White Pet'
Sempervirens Hybrid

Description: If a rose is to be grown on a terrace or balcony, it is usually a good idea to choose one that will give a continual display. This variety is just such an example, so it is surprising that it is not seen in catalogues more often. An excellent, low-level rose, it is covered with a multitude of superb clusters of small, salmon-pink flowers that last throughout the summer and into autumn.

Position: This rose is perfect for use in containers. The refined colour of its flowers harmonises well with Lady's Mantle, or perhaps a clump of gypsophila; a few white petunias will also work well as companions.

Description: If you are a fan of the Climber 'Félicité Perpétue', you will also like this rose, since it is the same but in miniature. Delightful little pink buds open out into small, double, pompon-like white blooms that are arranged in perfumed clusters. These will flower continuously until the autumn. The foliage is an elegant bluish-green.

Position: 'Little White Pet' is more than happy growing in a container, providing that you remember to feed it. It needs nourishment in order to flower well.

Characteristics

- **Height:** 60cm (24in)
- **Spread:** 60cm (24in)
- **Flowering:** repeat flowering
- **Pruning:** remove any clusters that have faded and cut back the branches at the end of winter

Characteristics

- **Height:** 50cm (20in)
- **Spread:** 45cm (18in)
- **Flowering:** repeat flowering
- **Pruning:** normal pruning at the end of winter

Roses for the balcony

'Bordure Nacrée'
Delbard 1963

Rosa nitida
North America 1807

Description: This is a rose of considerable charm. Its numerous, bushy branches and generous flowering habit make it especially suitable for growing in a pot or a planter. When they open out, the full double flowers are cream, almost yellow, in colour, changing to a pearly-white before taking on a pink tinge as they reach maturity. This rose has the added advantage of abundant foliage that remains disease-free, making it a fairly safe option.

Position: On a spacious terrace, 'Bordure Nacrée' would work well occupying a front-row position, with taller shrubs behind it, such as the summer-flowering blue ceanothus.

Description: Anyone wishing to create a fairly informal effect on their balcony or terrace might be glad of this rose. Its delightful fern-shaped leaves, born on prickly stems, are tinged with red in the autumn, just as some of the smaller maple trees. In the summer, its small but plentiful single flowers open out in a solid pink, arranged around highly visible golden stamens.

Position: Rosa nitida will tolerate light shade. Once the flowers have died off, its display will be renewed with a surprisingly attractive crop of elongated hips.

Characteristics

- **Height:** 40cm (16in)
- **Spread:** 40cm (16in)
- **Flowering:** repeat flowering
- **Pruning:** cut back short the oldest branches at the end of winter

Characteristics

- **Height:** 80cm (32in)
- **Spread:** 80cm (32in)
- **Flowering:** single flowering
- **Pruning:** not necessary – simply remove any dead wood on a regular basis

'Cécile Brünner'
Chinensis. Pernet-Ducher 1881

'The Fairy'
Polyantha. Bentall 1932

Description: 'Cécile Brünner's' flowers have a fresh, sweet perfume and are borne in loose clusters on dark green foliage. They are beautifully shaped in a lovely soft, shell-pink and flower throughout the summer and into autumn. This is a low-growing, miniature version of a Climber.

Position: This rose fits well in a garden border, while on a balcony it will thrive in a sunny position and look good positioned near white or dark blue perennial geraniums.

Description: This delightful rose is a popular inclusion in many catalogues. Large clusters of small, pompon-shaped flowers are carried on a dense bush with glossy foliage. Low-growing in habit, it flowers repeatedly from around mid-July into the autumn.

Position: It has its place in mixed borders, beds and low hedges, but is equally happy being grown in a container. This is also an excellent variety for use in bouquets.

Characteristics

- **Height:** 75cm (30in)
- **Spread:** 65cm (26in)
- **Flowering:** repeat flowering
- **Pruning:** at the end of winter

Characteristics

- **Height:** 60cm (24in)
- **Spread:** 80cm (32in)
- **Flowering:** repeat flowering
- **Pruning:** it is best to avoid pruning this rose in order to get the most from its attractive, natural shape

Roses for cutting

'Saint-Exupéry'
Delbard 2003

'Louise Odier'
Bourbon. Margottin 1851

Description: New flowers are created each year, and many are quickly forgotten. However, there is no likelihood of this happening to this creation, which boasts a number of positive features. First is the shape of the flower — it opens out of a pretty, round bud into a luxuriant and fully double bloom. Then there is the colour: a sumptuous and rich pink that will appeal to anyone who likes the colour of their roses warm. Finally, there is the perfume, which, not unnaturally, has a fragrance of roses and is truly splendid.

Position: An excellent rose for beds and borders. If you are feeling adventurous, you could plant it close to some chocolate cosmos or perennial sage with its shades of deep blue.

Characteristics

- **Height:** 80cm (32in)
- **Spread:** 65cm (26in)
- **Flowering:** repeat flowering
- **Pruning:** normal pruning at the end of winter

Description: The flowers of 'Louise Odier' may well remind you of the camellia. These velvet-like very full double blooms in shades of lilac give off a fragrant perfume and open out in generous clusters on a handsome, dense shrub. The branches bow attractively under the weight of the flowers and the warm colour of the blooms stands out against the beautiful, light green foliage. Although it merits inclusion in the section on the best pink roses, it has been included here because it looks superb in a lavish bouquet.

Position: This rose will look perfect in a mixed border, perhaps surrounded by delphiniums or clumps of sage.

Characteristics

- **Height:** 130cm (4ft 4in)
- **Spread:** 120cm (4ft)
- **Flowering:** repeat flowering
- **Pruning:** at the end of winter, cut back the weakest branches and prune the remaining stems to two or three buds

'Mamy Blue'
Delbard 1991

'Ingrid Bergman'
Hybrid Tea. Poulsen 1984

Description: This is another rose whose unusual colour – a sumptuous bluish-mauve – will bring a note of originality to a flowerbed or a bouquet. The blooms are very nicely shaped, and have a powerful perfume that carries notes of lemon balm, geraniums, violets and honey.

Position: Try combining 'Mamy Blue' with other roses of a flesh-pink or creamy-white colour, alongside some salmon- or raspberry-coloured Lady's Mantle.

Description: Among all the red roses that look equally good in the garden or in a bouquet, 'Ingrid Bergman' has to be one of the top choices. The petals in its full double blooms curl outwards in a vivid splash of colour against dense, dark green foliage. The flowers have a light perfume and repeat from June until the first frosts. Their long stems make them ideal for cutting.

Position: This rose will be at home in many different positions, from borders to massed beds. However, it is in a bouquet that its lovely blooms look their best.

Characteristics

- **Height:** 90cm (36in)
- **Spread:** 80cm (32in)
- **Flowering:** repeat flowering
- **Pruning:** normal pruning at the end of winter

Characteristics

- **Height:** 70cm (28in)
- **Spread:** 50cm (20in)
- **Flowering:** repeat flowering
- **Pruning:** normal pruning at the end of winter

Roses for cutting

'Michèle Meilland'
Meilland 1945

'Perle Noire'
Delbard 1986

Description: A perfect Hybrid Tea that flowers continuously. Its large, double blooms are an elegant, bright pink with hints of lilac that turn orangey in the centre. This is a reliable, uncomplicated rose with a very pleasant perfume and dark green foliage that remains resistant to disease.

Position: Flowers for cutting are usually best grown in beds. If planted in quantity, leave a space of 50cm (20in) between each plant. This rose can also be grown in a container.

Description: This magnificent dark red flower emerges from a black bud. Its perfect, sensuous blooms are borne on straight stems whose foliage is a uniform, plain green.

Position: 'Perle Noire' is *the* rose for bedding. Its blooms won't fade or change colour in the sunlight – indeed, a glint of sun will bring out its full beauty. Its excellent shape makes it an ideal flower for cutting.

Characteristics

- **Height:** 100cm (39in)
- **Spread:** 80cm (32in)
- **Flowering:** repeat flowering
- **Pruning:** cut back the branches to two or three buds at the end of winter

Characteristics

- **Height:** 100cm (39in)
- **Spread:** 90cm (36in)
- **Flowering:** repeat flowering
- **Pruning:** shorten the branches to two or three buds at the end of winter

'Sweet Juliet'
Austin 1989

'Terracotta'
Meilland

Description: With its light apricot colouring and its very elegant cup-shaped and fully double flowers, 'Sweet Juliet' fully deserves inclusion in this collection. A vigorous grower, this bushy rose produces excellent flowers for use in bouquets, with the sweet perfume that is typical of a Tea Rose. Its firm stems are complemented by shiny, medium-green foliage.

Position: This rose will look splendid when offset against a backdrop of Brazilian verbena in a mixed border. Care should be taken to plant it in rich soil and to keep the area well mulched.

Description: The deep tone of this rose is compelling, but seldom seen in the garden. Comprising about thirty petals, the flowers of 'Terracotta' contrast well against very thick foliage that has good resistance to disease.

Position: Plant this rose in a bed or border. Whether grown among other plants or cut for a bouquet, it will blend well with the bluish or silvery foliage of perennials, such as artemisia, iceplant or meadow-rue.

Characteristics

- **Height:** 100cm (39in)
- **Spread:** 90cm (36in)
- **Flowering:** repeat flowering
- **Pruning:** at the end of winter, prune the middle stems after removing any weak branches

Characteristics

- **Height:** 100cm (39in)
- **Spread:** 90cm (36in)
- **Flowering:** repeat flowering
- **Pruning:** normal pruning to two or three buds, at the end of winter

Curious and captivating

If you are on the lookout for something a little out of the ordinary, why not try a green rose, or a rose whose thorns make even more of a splash than its flowers. Or perhaps you are a slave to opulent and sensuous fragrance... in which case don't be ashamed to let yourself be led by your nose and try some of the suggestions on the following pages.

Unusual roses

Rosa foetida 'Bicolor'
Introduced c. 1590

Rosa sericea pteracantha
China. Introduced in 1890

Description: Also known as 'Austrian Copper' or 'Capucine Bicolore', this is a mutation of *Rosa foetida* ('Austrian Yellow'), which has golden-yellow flowers and blackish stems. *Rosa foetida* 'Bicolor' has single flowers of a handsome orangey-red with a yellow underside, but no fragrance. One plant may often produce both orange and yellow flowers, hence 'bicolour'.

Position: As it can be rather prone to black spot, this rose needs to be planted in a sheltered location. It looks spectacular planted on its own on a lawn, where its contrasting colours can really make a splash.

Description: Despite its pretty but small and discreet, single, white flowers with just four petals, this rose is known for its unusual thorns. Covering the length of its brown stems, they are large, transluscent and filled with a red sap. The effect is quite striking, particularly alongside the delicate, fern-like leaves. In early autumn, a crop of rounded hips adds to the display.

Position: From the point of view of the sheer size and quantity of its thorns, it would be hard to fault the choice of this rose for use in a hedge intended to act as a protective barrier.

Characteristics

- **Height:** 150cm (5ft)
- **Spread:** 150cm (5ft)
- **Flowering:** single flowering
- **Pruning:** after flowering, cut back by one-third

Characteristics

- **Height:** 300cm (10ft)
- **Spread:** 200cm (6ft 6in)
- **Flowering:** single flowering
- **Pruning:** prune out old wood regularly to encourage new growth

Rosa glauca
Europe 1830

Rosa chinensis 'Viridiflora'
Chinensis. 1833

Description: Also known as 'Rosa Rubrifolia' this Shrub Rose is grown for its lovely, blue-grey and purple foliage. Its small, single flowers are bright pink in colour, with white at the centre. They bloom at the start of summer, making way later for a crop of ornamental oval-shaped red hips.

Position: Plant several of these roses together, perhaps in a group of three, for a striking effect. Alternatively, plant one or two examples among other shrubs with contrasting foliage. A few euphorbias with pale green or bright orange bracts will work well at their base.

Description: A so-called 'black' rose is actually a very dark red in colour, but this rose, also known as 'the green rose' is definitely green. The petals of *Rosa chinensis* 'Viridiflora' have been replaced by green, dentate bracts with wine-coloured tinges. Resistant to disease, this rose fares best in sunny locations and in fertile soil.

Position: This rose is very much a curiosity. It is valued for its cut flowers in floral arrangements, but also when grown in the garden, as several of these plants can work well alongside slender perennials such as asters.

Characteristics

- **Height:** 200cm (6ft 6in)
- **Spread:** 150cm (5ft)
- **Flowering:** single flowering
- **Pruning:** simply cut out any dead wood if necessary

Characteristics

- **Height:** 95cm (36in)
- **Spread:** 70cm (28in)
- **Flowering:** repeat flowering
- **Pruning:** just a light prune at the end of the winter

Fragrant roses

'Sharifa Asma'
Austin 1983

'Roseraie de l'Haÿ'
Rugosa Hybrid. Cochet-Cochet 1901

Description: This lovely David Austin creation marries the delicacy of an Old Rose with the essential qualities of a Modern Rose. The shallow, cup-shaped flowers are flesh-pink, almost white, in colour, born on a short, compact bush with dense foliage. Their strong, fruity perfume is reminiscent of grapes and blackberries.

Position: The delicate paleness of its flowers is set off well against perennials with strong, contrasting colours, such as magenta-pink geraniums or the very elegant chocolate cosmos.

Description: When the large, flat, cup-shaped flowers on this sumptuous rose open out they are a pure crimson, but gradually darken as the blooms mature, taking on delicious, purplish tones. Its perfume is strong, opulent and sweet. In common with all members of the *Rugosa* family, 'Roseraie de l'Haÿ' has wrinkled leaves and spiny stems. It is a vigorous Shrub Rose that needs little attention.

Position: This rose will make a fragrant, informal hedge and fits well into a mixed border. It also looks particularly good next to a purple buddleia.

Characteristics
- **Height:** 110cm (42in)
- **Spread:** 100cm (39in)
- **Flowering:** repeat flowering
- **Pruning:** gentle pruning at the end of the winter

Characteristics
- **Height:** 120cm (4ft)
- **Spread:** 100cm (39in)
- **Flowering:** repeat flowering
- **Pruning:** light pruning at the end of winter

'Dioressence'
Hybrid Tea. Delbard-Chabert 1984

'Madame Isaac Pereire'
Bourbon. Garçon 1881

Description: This elegant rose arouses interest for its unique colour, bluish when in bud, giving way to an almost unreal pink, tinged with lilac. As might be expected from a name that carries more than a hint of a reference to the perfume industry, its fragrance is exceptional, mixing notes of bergamot, geraniums and moss, placing it up there with the very best of the new roses.

Position: Plant 'Dioressence' wherever you will have the opportunity to enjoy its perfume, or among perennials that are a soft pink or mauve to make an attractive colour combination.

Description: A sumptuous rose with very full double flowers in a lovely shade of dark crimson. Its perfume is opulent too, with slight peppery notes and a hint of raspberry. Once you come across this rose, you will be hooked. A robust Shrub Rose, its open habit and gently arching branches make it most attractive.

Position: Plant 'Madame Isaac Pereire' as a shrub or a Climber, but keep it close to pathways in order not to miss out on its rich fragrance.

Characteristics

- ■ **Height:** 90cm (36in)
- ■ **Spread:** 80cm (32in)
- ■ **Flowering:** repeat flowering
- ■ **Pruning:** normal pruning at the end of the winter

Characteristics

- ■ **Height:** 200cm (6ft 6in)
- ■ **Spread:** 200cm (6ft 6in)
- ■ **Flowering:** repeat flowering
- ■ **Pruning:** normal pruning at the end of the winter

Fragrant roses

'Rose de Rescht'

Damascena. Introduced by Nancy Lindsay at the end of the 1940s

'Ispahan'

Damascena. Before 1832

Description: When the blooms on this very full double Damask Rose open out they are a mauvish-pink, but deepen into a magenta-pink as they mature. However, it is not simply the depth of colour for which this rose is noteworthy, the reason for its inclusion in the list is its equally striking perfume. The flowers open out in elegant little clusters on an upright yet compact shrub with luxuriant foliage.

Position: In order to enjoy its delicate perfume to the full, grow this rose in a mixed border or in a bed that is not too far from pathways.

Description: During June, this handsome, vigorous and upright Shrub Rose is covered in a multitude of small, double flowers that are pale pink with tinges of lilac, with a strong, opulent perfume. They have good resistance to damage from heavy rain and are borne on foliage with an attractive blue tinge.

Position: Although single flowering, 'Ispahan' is a good rose to use in hedging, among perennials or growing in a container. Lasting several weeks, its flowering period is long enough to give it a good presence in the garden.

Characteristics

- **Height:** 90cm (36in)
- **Spread:** 75cm (30in)
- **Flowering:** regular repeat flowering after a first very abundant flowering in the summer
- **Pruning:** specialist grower Peter Beales recommends cutting this rose back extremely hard every five years

Characteristics

- **Height:** 130cm (52in)
- **Spread:** 120cm (48in)
- **Flowering:** single flowering
- **Pruning:** light pruning after flowering, but check for dead wood regularly and remove at the base

'Paul Ricard'
Hybrid Tea. Meilland 1991

'Yves Piaget'
Hybrid Tea. Meilland 1984

Description: A classic example of the Bush Rose, 'Paul Ricard' has a very marked aniseed fragrance and takes its name from the inventor of the French aniseed-flavoured drink. Its large, amber-yellow flowers open out at the tips of long stems, making them ideal for use in bouquets. The dense foliage is an elegant, matt green and shows excellent resistance to disease. If you are a fan of attractive, yellow roses that flower all summer and smell delightful, then look no further....

Position: Plant this rose in beds, borders or in a container. The lime-green flowers of Lady's Mantle would harmonise well.

Description: Although the pretty, frothy petals of 'Yves Piaget' give it the look of a peony, this rose does not suffer from the peony's fragility. It is a very robust shrub that flowers all summer long with a succession of intense, pink flowers with a powerful fragrance that borders on perfection.

Position: Plant this rose in any location that enables you to get close enough to smell its perfume: in beds and borders or in a bank, perhaps next to a large *Sedum spectabile* (iceplant), with which it will make an excellent combination

Characteristics

- **Height:** 100cm (39in)
- **Spread:** 90cm (36in)
- **Flowering:** repeat flowering
- **Pruning:** normal pruning at the end of the winter

Characteristics

- **Height:** 95cm (36in)
- **Spread:** 80cm (32in)
- **Flowering:** repeat flowering
- **Pruning:** normal pruning at the end of the winter

Fragrant roses

'André Le Nôtre'
Hybrid Tea. Meilland 1998

'O Sole Mio'
Hybrid Tea. Delbard

Description: Despite being a very recent creation, this rose resembles an Old Rose in many ways. It opens out into full, cup-shaped blooms that are pale pink with a slightly darker centre, borne on healthy, dense foliage. Even its opulent, delicious perfume is reminiscent of the varieties of yesteryear. It is hardly surprising that a French variety with so many plus points should be named after France's most celebrated gardener.

Position: This rose is ideal in a border or for use in bouquets.

Description: A Shrub Rose with large flowers, 'O Sole Mio' ranks among the best of Delbard's creations, even bordering on perfection. Borne on straight stems, the buds are in clusters of two or three and open out into flowers of a striking yellow with a rich, fruity perfume.

Position: Hybrid Teas are suitable for borders and beds. If planted in quantity, the effect can be quite spectacular. The lovely yellow of the flowers looks superb against the glossy foliage of a laurel hedge or the darker tones of clipped yew.

Characteristics

- **Height:** 100cm (39in)
- **Spread:** 90cm (36in)
- **Flowering:** repeat flowering
- **Pruning:** normal pruning at the end of the winter

Characteristics

- **Height:** 100cm (39in)
- **Spread:** 90cm (36in)
- **Flowering:** repeat flowering
- **Pruning:** normal pruning at the end of the winter

'Cuisse de Nymphe Émue'
Alba. Kew 1797

'Yolande d'Aragon'
Portland. Vibert 1843

Description: Otherwise known as 'Maiden's Blush', this rose bears flowers with petals so delicately crumpled that they almost seem to implore you to breathe in their fragrance, revealing a perfume that is both strong and sweet. It has dense, healthy foliage that is an attractive bluish-grey. Single flowering in late June, it also offers good resistance to disease.

Position: 'Cuisse de Nymphe Émue's' upright habit means that it works well in a hedge, but can also be a good choice for borders and beds.

Description: A popular rose thanks to large, very full double blooms that are a strong pink in colour, borne on straight stems on a vigorous, robust shrub. These lovely flowers, coupled with attractive, glossy foliage, mean that this rose has all the right ingredients to please even the most exacting rose-lover.

Position: Make the most of 'Yolande d'Aragon's' upright habit and plant it in a flowerbed or in a mixed border.

Characteristics

- **Height:** 180cm (6ft)
- **Spread:** 150cm (5ft)
- **Flowering:** : single flowering
- **Pruning:** prune lightly after flowering to remove any dead wood

Characteristics

- **Height:** 150cm (5ft)
- **Spread:** 120cm (4ft)
- **Flowering:** frequent repeat flowering
- **Pruning:** normal pruning at the end of the winter

Tough and robust

A collection of tough and resiliant roses, whose delicate appearance belies their robustness. Some are highly resistant to disease, while others will tolerate and even thrive in the more shady corners of the garden, or positively relish the opportunity to scramble up a north-facing wall. What more could one ask?

Roses tolerant of shade or semi-shade

'Albéric Barbier'
Luciae Hybrid. Barbier 1921

'Golden Showers'
Modern Hybrid. Lammerts 1956

Description: Bearing in mind the deep yellow buds that open out into large, full, creamy-white flowers with a yellowish centre and their strong and quite delicious perfume, it is hardly surprising that this Rambler is in all the catalogues. It also boasts glossy, green foliage and an iron constitution, being extremely tolerant of poor soil as well as shade and even able to flower profusely on a north-facing wall.

Position: Its long, supple branches are equally happy rambling over a pergola, a wall or even a mature tree.

Description: This is an excellent, straight-stemmed very popular Rambler with loosely formed, cup-shaped, double blooms that are golden-yellow veering towards cream. The flowers open out in clusters against dark, glossy foliage. This eye-catching rose can tolerate poor soil, and even positioned against a north-facing wall it should flower through to the first frosts.

Position: Train 'Golden Showers' against a wall or up a pillar or an arch, although it will look just as good in isolation on a lawn.

Characteristics

■ **Height:** 450cm (15ft)
■ **Spread:** 300cm (10ft)
■ **Flowering:** single flowering
■ **Pruning:** prune lightly after flowering

Characteristics

■ **Height:** 300cm (10ft)
■ **Spread:** 250cm (8ft 9in)
■ **Flowering:** repeat flowering
■ **Pruning:** at the end of the winter, lightly cut back the main branches and the secondary branches by about two-thirds of their length

'Blush Noisette'
Louis Noisette 1814

'Zéphirine Drouhin'
Bourbon. Bizot 1868

Description: This charming rose obligingly repeats its large clusters of small, double flowers with a fragrance of cloves. The flower heads are a pale pink, tinged with-lilac, revealing glimpses of their delicate stamens. This is a wonderfully informal, even 'rustic' shrub and very easy to look after.

Position: As this rose can manage perfectly well in a relatively shady position, it is used to brighten up the parts of the garden that are often neglected. It can be left to grow as a shrub or trained as a small Climber, in which case, try planting a clematis with medium-sized flowers or a lavender bush at its base.

Description: Blessed with an easy temperament and known for its lack of thorns (it is also called 'Thornless Rose') as well as having a particularly long flowering period, this rose has long been a favourite. Its semi-double blooms have an enchanting fragrance and are a mixture of carmine and cherry-red.

Position: Another rose that grows well, even in less than ideal situations, providing that it has plenty of space around it. It will flower even in a north-facing situation if the shade is not too deep. Grow it either as a Climber or as a shrub.

Characteristics
- **Height:** 250cm (8ft 9in)
- **Spread:** 220cm (8ft 3in)
- **Flowering:** repeat flowering
- **Pruning:** at the end of the winter

Characteristics
- **Height:** 250cm (8ft 9in)
- **Spread:** 200cm (6ft 6in)
- **Flowering:** repeat flowering
- **Pruning:** normal pruning at the end of the winter

Roses tolerant of shade or semi-shade

'Félicité et Perpétue'
Sempervirens Hybrid. Jacques 1827

'Madame Alfred Carrière'
Noisette. Schwartz 1879

Description: A profusion of small, fully double flowers hang in drooping clusters on this rose. It has handsome, glossy foliage that is virtually evergreen and almost entirely lacking in thorns. The red-tipped buds develop into creamy-white blooms that give off an attractive fragrance. This rose flowers only once in the season, but it would be a great shame to discount it just for that reason.

Position: Providing that it has a solid means of support – such as a pergola, arch or tree – this Rambler grows well everywhere, and even poor soil or a semi-shaded position will not spoil its obliging nature.

Description: Pretty flowers in small, milky-white clusters tinged with pale pink are combined with a very fragrant, almost fruity perfume in a winning combination. The branches are long and smooth, practically without thorns, supporting lovely, glossy, pale green foliage.

Position: This is an ideal Climber – it is vigorous, with supple branches that are easy to train. It will even take a north-facing position, where it flowers only slightly less profusely.

Characteristics
- **Height:** 400cm (13ft)
- **Spread:** 400cm (13ft)
- **Flowering:** single flowering
- **Pruning:** prune after flowering

Characteristics
- **Height:** 450cm (15ft)
- **Spread:** 300cm (10ft)
- **Flowering:** repeat flowering
- **Pruning:** normal pruning at the end of the winter

'Narrow Water'
Moschata Hybrid. Daisyhill 1883

'Splendens'
Arvensis Hybrid. Before 1837

Description: This very pretty rose has semi-double flowers of a pale lilac-pink with attractive, visible stamens gathered into small clusters. The flowers give off a perfume that is both opulent and gentle. The dark, matt foliage provides an attractive backdrop for the handsome, small, coral-coloured buds, and is highly resistant to disease.

Position: This is an easy-going rose that can adapt itself to a variety of circumstances. Grown as a bush, it can easily be introduced into a hedge, or placed in a mixed border alongside other shrubs. It can also be trained as a low Climber against small walls, fences or pergolas, and will adapt itself without difficulty to a shady position.

Description: Who would guess that 'Splendens' pretty, rounded, reddish little buds would open out into large, cup-shaped, white flowers with a slight rose tint in their petals? Often grown as a shrub, this handsome bush with its supple, reddish branches can also be trained as a Climber. Its clusters of flowers give off a delicious perfume reminiscent of myrrh.

Position: Combine 'Splendens' with peonies, irises or centaury to create a wonderfully romantic corner in the garden.

Characteristics

- **Height:** 250cm (8ft 9in)
- **Spread:** 200cm (6ft 6in)
- **Flowering:** repeat flowering
- **Pruning:** at the end of the winter, cut back the side shoots to two or three buds

Characteristics

- **Height:** 400cm (13ft)
- **Spread:** 250cm (8ft 9in)
- **Flowering:** single flowering
- **Pruning:** cut back if necessary after flowering

Tough and resiliant roses

'De la Grifferaie'
Multiflora Hybrid. Vibert 1845

'Belle Poitevine'
Rugosa Hybrid. Bruant 1894

Description: This rose's reputation for robustness is entirely justified and has made it a long-time favourite source of rootstock for Standard Roses. It is less common in catalogues nowadays, possibly because of its inevitable presence in old-style garden planting schemes. My personal view is that its fully double, magenta-pink flowers, excellent perfume and handsome, disease-free foliage make it well worth the attention of anyone looking for a rose that is easy to grow.

Position: 'De la Grifferaie's' vivid blooms can be used to brighten up a number of locations. With its large flower clusters, it looks particularly striking against a background of vine-leaves or ivy.

Description: This handsome shrub bears all the hallmarks of a *Rugosa*, hence it is a luxuriant, particularly vigorous rose that is easy to grow. Its pointed buds open out into large, pretty, semi-double flowers that are pink-magenta in colour. A well-balanced shrub made up of relatively angular stems, it bears attractive, orange hips in the autumn.

Position: Combine three prominent members of the *Rugosa* family, 'Belle Poitevine', 'Blanc double de Coubert' and 'Roseraie de l'Haÿ', to create a hedge full of white, pink and red flowers.

Characteristics

- **Height:** 300cm (10ft)
- **Spread:** 250cm (8ft 9in)
- **Flowering:** single flowering
- **Pruning:** remove the oldest branches at the base regularly

Characteristics

- **Height:** 180cm (6ft)
- **Spread:** 150cm (5ft)
- **Flowering:** good repeat flowering in the autumn
- **Pruning:** at the end of the winter

'Baltimore Belle'
Setigera Hybrid. Feast 1843

'Gipsy Boy'
Bourbon. Lambert 1909

Description: The main characteristic of this handsome Rambler is the veritable harvest of small, pale pink flowers with a very pleasing perfume that are borne in large clusters. The flowering period is longer than for most single flowering roses and the foliage is highly resistant to disease.

Position: This rose grows quite happily in light shade where the fresh colour of its petals will brighten up any shady spot. If grown over an arch, the delicate droop of its pretty blooms makes an attractive display.

Description: The easy-going nature of this 'gipsy' helps it to adapt happily to difficult conditions. Its double blooms are a strong crimson with contrasting primrose-yellow stamens at the centre. The flowers have a pleasant, light perfume.

Position: Completely hardy, this rose will grow in comfort in a semi-shaded position. If grown as a Climber, it can reach a height of 3m (10ft) or more, and it can also be grown as a shrub. Its lovely colour looks superb against purple-leaved shrubs such as the splendid *Cotinus coggygria* 'Royal Purple' (Smokebush).

Characteristics

- **Height:** 400cm (13ft)
- **Spread:** 300cm (10ft)
- **Flowering:** single flowering
- **Pruning:** shorten the stems after flowering

Characteristics

- **Height:** 180cm (6ft)
- **Spread:** 150cm (5ft)
- **Flowering:** single flowering
- **Pruning:** cut back after flowering, removing any dead wood

Tough and resiliant roses

'Thérèse Bugnet'
Rugosa Hybrid. Bugnet 1950

Rosa gallica 'Officinalis'
Brought back from the crusades by Thibaut IV of Champagne c. 1250

Description: It's difficult not to succumb to the charms of these large, perfumed, double flowers borne on reddish stems. Perfect little deep crimson buds open out into blooms that become progressively paler as they mature and are beautifully set off by the extremely robust, pale green foliage. The *Rugosa* family antecedents of this gem of a rose have also endowed it with an excellent perfume.

Position: Perfectly happy growing in a semi-shady position, this rose can be used to create hedging that will remain in flower until the first frosts, or will look splendid grown in a small group of three on a lawn.

Description: This is the famous 'Provins Rose', also known as the 'Apothecary's Rose', and adopted as the Red Rose of Lancaster in the 15th century. It is equally renowned for its perfume about which much has been written. The brilliant, crimson-red, semi-double flowers come into bloom in June, while in autumn, small, orangey-red hips make a lovely ornamental display and are much appreciated by the birds.

Position: This rose looks at its best in a mixed border in a relatively informal setting. Plant it near a path or a sitting area to gain the most benefit from its fragrance.

Characteristics

- **Height:** 180cm (6ft)
- **Spread:** 180cm (6ft)
- **Flowering:** repeat flowering
- **Pruning:** prune hard at the end of the winter

Characteristics

- **Height:** 150cm (5ft)
- **Spread:** 120cm (4ft)
- **Flowering:** single flowering
- **Pruning:** moderate pruning after flowering

'Mrs John Laing'
Repeat flowering Hybrid. Bennet 1887

'Pink Grootendorst'
Rugosa Hybrid. Grootendorst 1923

Description: This lovely, repeat flowering hybrid displays elongated buds followed by very full double blooms borne on long stems. The pale pink hue of the flowers is lifted by the robust, grey-green foliage, while the fragrance given off by the flowers is both sweet and opulent.

Position: With its vigorous, upright foliage, this useful shrub is able to suit a number of locations, from borders and mixed beds to containers on terraces and balconies, where its long flowering season makes it popular choice.

Description: With its frilly petals a fresh shade of pink, the small, double blooms of this rose look more like carnations than roses. They are borne in clusters and repeat flower continuously until the autumn. Taken as a whole, this is not the most elegant looking of the Shrub Roses, but it is very hardy with dense foliage that is disease-free.

Position: Plant 'Pink Grootendorst' in a border, or close to the house as the flowers are excellent for cutting (although they have no perfume), or even use it to form a hedge.

Characteristics

- **Height:** 120cm (4ft)
- **Spread:** 100cm (39in)
- **Flowering:** repeat flowering
- **Pruning:** at the end of the winter

Characteristics

- **Height:** 150cm (5ft)
- **Spread:** 120cm (4ft)
- **Flowering:** repeat flowering
- **Pruning:** hard pruning is required at the end of the winter

Roses in the garden

The traditional rose garden

As with house interiors, garden design is subject to the vagaries of fashion. Some people prefer to display their roses in a formal setting, in traditional rose beds, while others consider this the epitome of poor taste. Roses are often planted at the edge of a lawn so that they can be seen from the house, and in this type of arrangement, the Hybrid Teas and the Floribundas – both intended to draw the eye for as long as possible – reign supreme. A quick trawl through the catalogues and you will find that they are full of mouth-watering, eye-catching ideas.

Taste and colour

Formal rose beds were very much in vogue back in the 1970s, and had it not been for this fashion, some varieties, such as 'Queen Elizabeth' (Lammerts, USA 1954), would probably never have achieved such popularity. Nowadays, although many gardeners prefer to see a more informal planting scheme in which herbaceous plants and other shrubs are combined with roses, the traditional rose bed still holds its appeal. Those not in favour of the traditional approach might point out the unattractive look of the strips of bare earth between rows of dormant rose bushes throughout the winter months. While others might dislike the effect of formally-arranged rows of bright yellow or red flowers clashing loudly with the soft green of the lawn. But it's all just a matter of taste.

How about a border?

To define the edge of a rose bed you could plant – depending on the climate – some low box hedging, lavender or *Santolina* (cotton lavender). These evergreens will liven up the bed with their foliage during the winter and will then provide an attractive colour contrast in the flowering season. Box and cotton lavender require pruning twice each season. Lavender should be pruned after it has finished flowering, but be careful not to touch the woody parts, which may otherwise not recover.

Pictured left:
'Perle Noire', 'Grüss an Aachen',
'Paul Ricard', 'William Shakespeare 2000'

Practicalities

Planting a border

To create a massed effect, roses need to be planted in three or four rows, either aligned or staggered, and spaced 40–60cm (16–24in) apart depending upon the predicted spread of the chosen variety. After planting, apply a thick peat or pine-bark mulch to keep weeds at bay (see page 27).

Which roses to choose

Rose beds, by definition, are always very much on display, so repeat flowering roses are best. Hybrid Teas and Floribundas are recommended.

■ **Pink roses:** 'Queen Elizabeth', 'Fêtes Galantes', 'Heritage' or 'William Shakespeare 2000'
■ **White roses:** 'Iceberg' or 'Grüss an Aachen'
■ **Red roses:** 'Papa Meilland', 'Lili Marlène', 'Hacienda' or 'Perle Noire'
■ **Yellow roses:** 'Paul Ricard' or 'Violin d'Ingres' (Meilland)

Rose hedging

Roses can prove extremely useful for separating sections of the garden or to create a boundary with a neighbouring property. The choice is so vast that it is sometimes hard to know where to begin, not to mention which are the varieties best suited to each location. Deciding factors will be the desired height and shape.

Low hedging or informal hedging

If you want to use a low, straight hedge about 100–150cm (3–5ft) high to separate one part of the garden from another, then cluster-flowering Bush Roses (*R. floribunda*) provide the ideal solution. If, on the other hand, you prefer an informal hedge with a more natural look, choose roses from the *Rugosa* family, or perhaps older strains, whose thorny branches will give you, in time, an impenetrable screen that could stand 200–250cm (6ft 6in–8ft 9in) high.

How to prune a rose hedge *(see also pages 30-35)*

The first year

Newly-planted roses (those planted in spring or the previous autumn or winter) should always be pruned hard to encourage the growth of side shoots at the base of the plant. After that, only Bush Roses need to be cut back hard each year.

Old Roses and Botanical Roses

In the first two years, the branches of Old Roses and Botanical Roses should be cut back hard. From the third year onwards, they simply need tidying-up, without touching their overall natural shape.

Single flowering roses

These should be pruned just after they have flowered. This allows new branches to grow that will bear flowers the following year.

Pictured left:
Rosa alba 'Semiplena', 'Goldbusch', 'Rush'

Practicalities

Planting a hedge

To make a low hedge, plant roses in rows, spaced about 50cm (20in) apart. For a thick hedge, plant a second row about 30cm (12in) in front of the previous row, still spaced about 50cm (20in) apart, but staggered with the first row.

For an informal hedge, plant the roses in a single row, with a little space between them: allow 100–120cm (39–48in). As the plants fill out, they will form a protective barrier.

Planting distances will vary according to the type of hedging and density required, and the type of rose selected.

Which roses to choose

■ For low hedging that is attractive and full of flowers, try 'Lavender Dream' (Interplant 1984) or 'Centenaire de Lourdes' (Delbart-Chabert 1958).

■ For a more informal, wilder-looking hedge, refer to the pages covering hedging roses, single flowering roses or Bush Roses and try 'Nevada', 'Rush', 'Stanwell Perpetual' or the delightful 'Joséphine de Beauharnais'.

A rose corridor

If you want to link different parts of the garden or create a pretty path leading to the house, it is fairly easy to install a series of arches that can support a profusion of climbing roses. It is important to think in advance about the amount of weight they will have to support and to take into account also likely wear and tear caused by bad weather.

A path for all seasons

A narrow border beside a path can be enhanced by some tried and tested flower combinations planted among the roses – try irises, peonies, nepetas, Lady's Mantle or some lovely perennial geraniums. At the beginning of spring, and before the first rose blooms appear, a path can be brightened up with spring-flowering bulbs such as snowdrops, grape hyacinths, narcissi, daffodils, scillas and tulips. In winter, some neatly trimmed box bushes and variegated ivy chosen for its delicate foliage will hold interest. A dedicated gardener should never be daunted by the dormant season.

Building an arch

Old rose arches may still be found at some garden reclamation yards, but they are often very expensive. Arches made of metal or plastic are now readily available from garden centres. If you don't mind a spot of DIY, you could also consider making your own framework out of wood. Use posts that are a minimum of 10cm (4in) in diameter and attach a piece of trellis, or wires fixed horizontally approximately every 40cm (16in). It's worth remembering to apply a timber preservative to the posts and before sinking them (deep enough) into the soil. A depth of 60cm (2ft) is about right, setting them in concrete if necessary. An even simpler solution would be to use flexible metal rods that could be bent over to form an arch, but the ends need to be firmly fixed into the ground.

Pictured left:
'Mermaid', New Dawn, 'Paul Transon'

Practicalities

Handy to know

Arches that can be purchased at garden centres and DIY stores also offer a variety of possible options.

Tips

■ Consider planting a mix of bulbs and perennials, as well as adding a few annuals, to keep the border to your path looking lovely all year round.

■ A mixture of repeat and single flowering roses is a good combination. Alternatively, single flowering roses can easily accommodate one or two large-flowered clematis, which will attract a lot of attention when they come into bloom in mid- or late summer.

Which roses to choose

Countless varieties can be used on arches and pergolas. It is obviously tempting to go for repeat flowering roses, to take full advantage of their long flowering season.

■ 'Zéphirine Drouhin', a pink rose, and 'Madame Alfred Carrière', which is pearly-white, are good choices due to their supple stems and excellent resistance to disease.

■ It would, however, be a pity to ignore some of the single flowering varieties, which put on a tremendous display once they come into bloom. Once such example is 'Constance Spry', which produces an avalanche of large, round, pale pink flowers with a delicious scent of myrrh.

Covering walls and mature trees

Garden walls and fences in a garden are a real godsend for the rose lover. The front of a house is also a tempting site, and if the flowers are fragrant, on a soft summer's day an intoxicating perfume will float into the house through open windows.

Good trees for roses

A Rambling Rose is an excellent way to add interest to a mature tree or a conifer that has begun to look jaded. However, don't plant them too close to the trunk where the soil will be very dry, especially in the case of a conifer. Old fruit trees can also be given a new lease of life, thanks to the profuse flowering habit of Ramblers and as an added bonus, the latter need no attention at all – apart from a quick trim with the shears if it looks as though they are becoming invasive. Most Ramblers also produce a handsome display of autumn hips, which will be much appreciated by the birds before the onset of winter.

A question of orientation

The orientation of the facade or wall against which a rose is grown also plays a large part in its success. East- and west-facing walls are the best, whereas against a south-facing wall a rose may suffer from too much heat, so make sure you water and regular feed it regularly. If planted against a north-facing wall, cold and lack of sunshine may get the better of your rose. Whatever the case, some roses are more adept than others at thriving in less-than-ideal conditions, but the catalogues usually make this clear. A selection of roses that tolerate shade or semi-shade can be found on pages 114–117.

Pictured left:
'Paul's Himalayan Musk', 'Bleu Magenta', Pierre de Ronsard'

Practicalities

Construct a framework

To construct a framework against a wall, hammer in nails or pegs with an eye at one end. These will enable you to attach a network of wires along which the roses can be trained. Space the wires 30–40cm (12–16in) apart and be sure to leave a gap of about 3cm (a good inch) between the wire and the wall to allow the stems to grow around and behind the wires. (See also page 20.)

Take care when planting

A rose should not be planted less than 30cm (12in) from the foot of a wall, since the soil here is generally of poor quality and often dry. Place a mixture of compost and bonemeal at the bottom of the planting hole, making sure that the roots of the rose are well fanned out and directed away from the wall. Water copiously after planting is completed. (See also page 20.)

Choosing your rose

A number of varieties of rose can be trained against a wall. You will want to bear in mind, of course, the colour and fragrance, but also the vigour of the rose and whether or not it will repeat flower. The heights given in catalogues will allow you to get an idea of the size of the plant at maturity. It would be a mistake, for example, to plant a Climber that can reach a height of 10m (33ft) against a low wall or the side of a small building.

Tips

■ Roses that are planted against a wall must be fed well.
■ An east- or west-facing orientation is best.
■ Choose Rambling Roses to grow up trees.
■ Make sure the supporting framework is strong enough.
■ Train the branches in the direction in which you want them to grow.

In the kitchen garden

Kitchen gardens are coming back into fashion once more, and nowadays, people are growing a few herbs and a couple of rows of lettuces or radishes in even the tiniest patches of ground. Roses have always fitted in well here, along with irises or dahlias, or with one or two Climbers planted alongside espalier-trained fruit trees. Previous generations built walls around their kitchen gardens to protect their crops against wind chill, but nowadays building a wall is less common. Instead, people are enclosing their kitchen gardens with hornbeams, willow, box hedging or clipped yew, or even a wooden fence.

Roses at harvest time

It is such a delight when you head down to the kitchen garden to pick the season's first crop of peas to be greeted by clusters of fragrant roses. If yours is an old garden and you are lucky enough to have a well, then 'Ghislaine de Féligonde' with its charming, pompon-shaped apricot-yellow flowers will fit in nicely. A Ground-cover Rose such as 'Nozomi' or 'Kent' looks good just encroaching over the edges of flagstones or paved areas, or perhaps trailing near a water butt, and will brighten the place up into October. The choice is huge, in every colour, and many have excellent resistance to disease.

Make a splash at the entrance

If your garden is big enough to enable you to devote a section of it to fruit and vegetables, a highly attractive way to demarcate the two sections is by a gate over which a single rose is cascading. Choose from a range of roses which will be in keeping with the relatively informal setting, such as 'Dorothy Perkins', with its small, double, pompon-shaped crimson flowers, or 'Apple Blossom', which is a vigorous Rambler with single, pale pink flowers that have a light perfume.

Pictured left:
'Comte de Chambord', 'Nevada', 'Ballerina'

Practicalities

Tips
- Try planting an unfussy Climber at the entrance to the kitchen garden.
- Standard Roses can work well in contrast to the rounded shape of some vegetables.
- Choose roses with a graceful, curved shape rather than Hybrid Teas, for example, which look too elegant in a kitchen garden setting.

Standard Roses among the vegetables

If space allows, plant two Standard Roses in the kitchen garden, or even two Weeping Standards on either side of the entrance to a pathway. Similarly, a very delicate variety such as 'Félicité et Perpetué' will look very pretty positioned at the intersection of several paths. Dress up the soil around the foot of Standards with aromatic herbs such as sage, thyme or marjoram.

A perfumed area

Most rose-lovers have a penchant for fragrance and are unlikely to be satisfied unless at least a small corner of their garden is perfumed by roses. Many people make a point of selecting roses for their fragrance and build up collections of the sweetest smelling varieties. Specialist rose-growers are well aware of this and devote much of their time towards creating new varieties that, as far as possible, combine beauty with unusual and alluring fragrances. If the space you have is limited, make this type of rose your first choice.

The finest fragrances

The André Eve catalogue suggests combining 'Rose de Rescht', 'Yolande d'Aragon', 'Enfant de France', 'Charles Mills' and 'Cuisse de Nymphe', all of which have raspberry notes. Delbard's new creation 'Saint-Exupéry' would go extremely well near 'Chartreuse de Parme', which has won a number of prizes for its heady perfume. These two roses go very well with 'Grand Siècle', which has an extremely delicate colour and an exquisite perfume. The 'Generosa' series by Guillot combines a delicious fragrance with an exceptional flowering capability, while 'Paul Ricard', 'Papa Meilland' and 'André le Nôtre' offer just a glimpse of the hundreds of delicious varieties available from French grower Meilland. When it comes to English roses, David Austin has firmly established his reputation – his 'William Shakespeare 2000' brings together an Old Rose perfume and a sublime shade of deep red, and his 'Evelyn', a blend of apricot and peach, gives off a highly subtle, fruity note.

A matter of personal taste

We all have our favourite perfumes, but if you are not sure which roses correspond to your taste, stroll around some established rose gardens and nurseries with a notebook and pen and breathe in! After a few such outings, you will soon be able to put together your ideal, rose-perfumed garden.

Pictured left:
'Madame Isaac Perèire', 'O sole mio', 'Cuisse de Nymphe émue'

Practicalities

Planting suggestions

■ To benefit most from their fragrance, plant roses near to paths or places where you sit out on fine days. If you plant three of the same variety in a group, not only will the roses make a striking display, their perfume will smell even stronger.

■ Another idea is to position them in a geometric shape – perhaps a square or a rectangle – in a sunny, sheltered spot, and have fun bringing together roses with complementary perfumes. Of course, you should take care to avoid any colour clashes.

■ Alternatively, create two long, rectangular beds with a narrow strip of lawn between them. Position an old, rustic-looking seat at the far end on which you can sit and enjoy your collection in peace.

Tips

■ Draw up the plant list for your perfumed garden with the aid of catalogues and after having made a few exploratory outings to established gardens.

■ Ideally, try to position your perfumed area near to where people will walk.

■ Plant in groups and take care to keep your colours harmonised.

The white garden

At Sissinghurst in Kent, there is a fabulous white garden that has remained a model of its kind. The magnificent Rambling Rose planted by Vita Sackville-West still dominates the garden. If it is difficult for you to recreate this look in your own garden because it is used for many different purposes and by different family members, why not make just a portion of it themed, delineated perhaps by a low hedge.

The many shades of white

Study a white flower closely and you may find that it is not pure white. White flowers can have tinges of any colour from amber to green or from pink to yellow. If you would like to create a white rose bed, try combining 'Iceberg', 'Madame Alfred Carrière', 'Ice Cream', 'Margaret Merril' and 'Blanc double de Coubert'. When buying, remember to also take into consideration the overall shape and growing habit of the rose.

Shrubs to accompany white roses

Shrubs with a hint of silver in the foliage work well (*Pyrus salicifolia* 'Pendula' [or 'Weeping Pear'] is particularly good), as do buddleias or *Hebes* with grey- or silver-toned leaves. There are also a number of white-flowered shrubs, including *Viburnum*, *Deutzia*, *Seringa* (Philadelphus), or lilac (go for *Syringa vulgaris* 'Madame Lemoine' and 'Madame Abel Chantenay', which have creamy-white flowers). Think about planting evergreens too, so that your white garden doesn't look too bare in the winter. Yews and variegated or plain English holly will help to bulk out the box plants. As soon as spring is in the air, tulips, narcissi and white hyacinths can help to start the display.

Pictured left:
'Iceberg', 'Prosperity', 'Sombreuil'.

Practicalities

Getting everything to match

■ Spend a little time studying catalogues or visiting gardens, noting down the names of any plants that will blend well with your roses.
■ White perennials include lupins, poppies, campanulas, carnations, geraniums, irises, gypsophila, camomiles, scabious and Japanese anemones. An interesting addition would be *Crambe cordifolia* (Giant Seakale), which is spectacular when its flowers open out in a pure white cloud, and often reaches a height of 200cm (6ft 6in).
■ The success of the garden will hinge on the combination of flowers with foliage, which is an essential factor in this type of project. Any silver-leafed plant will come in useful – artemisia, *Stachys byzantina* (Silver Carpet or Lamb's Ears) and white lavender, for example. Planted anywhere near white roses that have a yellow tinge, Lady's Mantle looks tremendous, as do some *Hostas*. A variegated sage will also work well.

Tips

■ Silver and grey foliage play an important part in a white garden.
■ Plant your roses in groups of three for greater effect.

Roses and shrubs

Shrubs make the ideal accompaniment for roses. They are also used increasingly often to give added value to a bed or to fill the gaps between the short flowering seasons of their more showy neighbours.

Which shrubs to choose

When choosing shrubs to plant with your roses, take into account the colour of the flowers and the actual flowering period. Viburnums, which can be white, pinkish-white or plain pink, and mainly come into flower in April and May, look equally splendid in autumn, when their foliage turns red and their branches are covered in gleaming berries. Also providing a particularly interesting foil for roses are *Kolwitzia, Deutzia, Daphne, Ceanothus, Weigelia* and *Philadelphus*. Think about how each plant is likely to develop, in order to keep a good balance of shapes and sizes. Varieties that will grow larger should be planted at the back of the border – or at the centre, if the bed will be viewed from all sides.

Roses and clematis

A great many gardens nowadays combine roses with clematis, and the results always look splendid if you make the right choice of colours. 'Blanc Double de Coubert' and the pale mauve clematis 'Victoria' go very well together. In the same way, a combination of pink roses and dark purple clematis (such as Clematis viticella 'Blue Bells') is particularly successful.

Another option is to allow a clematis to grow through single flowering Shrub Roses or Climbers, as they will bloom in summer and compensate for the roses' lack of repeat flowering.

The buds on most summer-flowering clematis flower on the current year's growth, which means that they can be pruned back at the end of the winter to about 70cm (28in) from the base.

The number of clematis varieties available is huge and you may find the choice bewildering, It pays, therefore, to do a little research before you buy, in order to arrive at the best mix of colours and bring some extra interest to single flowering roses.

Pictured left:
'Marguerite Hilling', 'Complicata', Tuscany Superb'

Practicalities

Choose the right colours

■ Purple-leaved shrubs provide a lovely contrast to white, pink or dark red roses. Examples of these shrubs include some types of *Prunus*, ornamental apple trees, berberis (*Berberis* 'Atropurpurea') or the dramatic Smokebush (*Cotinus coggygria* 'Royal Purple').
■ For an excellent complement to yellow, orange or bright red roses, think about using the variegated foliage of some hollies and weigelias, or privet.

Handy to know

White, pink and dark red roses look good with certain colour tones. Yellow, orange or bright red roses, on the other hand, are a different group with different requirements.

When you are selecting roses and shrubs to plant close to each other, check up on their flowering seasons as well as the colour of their blooms.

Roses and perennials

The idea of combining roses and perennials together in a herbaceous border is hardly a new one, but it proves its worth time and again. It used to be thought that roses did not mix well with other plants, but this has long been disproved and many roses can be used in a mixed bed or border to great effect.

Small efforts and large rewards

Creating a mixed border can be daunting unless you have plenty of time to spare. Fortunately, even if you are working on a small scale, combining roses and perennials produces satisfying results very quickly and can also give a whole new feel to a garden. Introduce just one or two roses at first, taking into consideration the height the plants will attain at maturity. Don't space the plants too far apart, so that when they come into bloom, the flowers will blend in together.

A marriage of opposites

Yellow, orange or bright red roses look good against a striking contrast, so choose perennials such as yellow achilleas (yarrow), copper-toned euphorbias, rudbeckias, saxifrages, scarlet crocosmias and golden rod. However, this list is far from exhaustive, so go ahead and experiment. Whatever happens, if the result isn't exactly what you had in mind, you can easily rethink your scheme the following year.

Pictured left:
'Heritage', 'Cardinal de Richelieu', 'Centenaire de Lourdes'

Practicalities

Tips

■ Decide in advance what result you want to achieve.

■ The number of permutations is endless, so choose your colours according to whether you want strong contrasts or matching tones.

■ It's important to take into account the growing habit of a rose before making your choice of perennials to accompany it. Hybrid Teas (or other large-bloomed varieties) will sit more comfortably alongside plainer border plants (such as box, santolina or lavender) than Old Roses, which can be made less heavy by evening primrose or clouds of gypsophila.

■ A flowerbed does not need to be large in order to be effective.

■ Remember to consider the flowering seasons when choosing your plants.

Roses and thyme

They say that aromatic plants keep bugs and parasites away from your rose bushes. If that's the case, why not mix business with pleasure and plant some sage, thyme and rosemary among your roses. Even mint is useful, although it's invasive, or you could think about bergamot (also known as beebalm), which brings beautiful bursts of colour. And if you find that the ants and the greenfly decide to stay put despite all your efforts, at least you will have created a pretty little corner.

Classic combinations

■ Geraniums, Lady's Mantle and various types of nepeta are commonly used alongside roses. These look marvellous when planted below some varieties of Bush Roses or Climbing Roses, which, as they mature, can often lose their leaves. As well as filling a gap, they keep the area cool and prevent the soil from compacting.

■ If your rose bushes have grown rather tall, delphiniums will not look out of place. And you can boost your display of some early-flowering varieties with irises and tulips, which come up each year.

Inspiring plant combinations
for your garden

Border tones

1 *Cosmos sulphurous* (orange cosmos)

2 *Arundo donax* 'Variegata' (variegated giant grass)

3 *Hemerocallis fulva* 'Kwanso Flore Plena' (orange daylily)

4 *Rosa* 'Graham Thomas'

5 *Crocosmia* 'Lucifer' (montbretia)

6 *Kniphofia uvaria* (red-hot poker)

7 *Euphorbia griffithii* 'Fireglow' (euphorbia or milkwort)

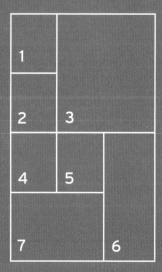

Pure white

1 *Rosa* 'Winchester Cathedral'

2 *Artemisia ludoviciana* 'Valerifinnis' (artemisia or mugwort)

3 *Selinum wallichianum* (cow-parsley)

4 and **5** *Anemone x hybrida* 'Honorine Jobert' (Japanese anemone)

6 *Clematis* 'Mme Lecoultre' (clematis)

7 *Paeonia lactiflora* (white peony)

Purple tones

1 *Leycesteria Formosa* (Himalayan honeysuckle)

2 and **3** *Amaranthus* 'Magic Fountain' (Love-lies-bleeding)

4 *Berberis auricoma* (barberry)

5 *Rosa glauca* (Shrub Rose)

6 *Knautia macedonica* (knautia or Macedonian scabious)

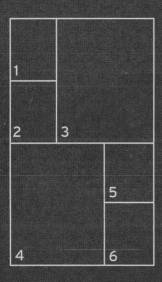

In classic mood

1 *Lupinus albus L.* (white lupin)

2 *Rosa* 'Comte de Chambord'

3 *Delphinium* 'Faust'

4 *Borago* (white borage)

5 *Digitalis purpurea* (foxglove)

6 *Lavatera cachemiriana* (tree mallow)

7 *Cynara cardunculus* (artichoke thistle or cardoon)

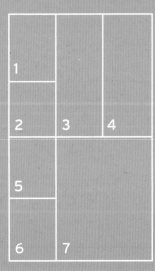

Against a wall

1 *Paeonia* 'Sarah Bernhardt' (peony)

2 *Philadelphus* (mock orange)

3 *Kolwitzia amabilis* (beautybush)

4 *Nepeta* 'Six Hills Grant' (catmint)

5 *Rosa* 'Constance Spry'

6 *Achillea millefolium* 'Lilac Beauty' (yarrow)

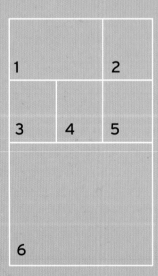

appendices

Complete list of varieties

Single flowering varieties

These roses flower just once in summer, but are so spectacular that they should not be overlooked. The list includes a number of old varieties, whose beauty is unmatched.

Repeat flowering varieties

From May through to October, many of the following will delight you by their more or less continuous flowering. The greater the effort you put into dead-heading, the longer they will bloom.

Where to buy the best roses

David Austin Roses

Bowling Green Lane
Albrighton, Wolverhampton
WV7 3HB
Tel 01902 376300
Fax 01902 372142

www.davidaustinroses.com

David Austin sells over 900 rose varieties from his nursery based in the midlands. He has recently opened a plant centre where some 300 different varieties of container-grown roses are for sale as well as many other plants. There is also a two-acre garden where you can see many hundreds of rose varieties growing in situ.

Peter Beales Roses

London Road, Attleborough
Norwich, Norfolk
NR17 1AY
Tel 01953 454707
Fax 01953 456845

www.classicroses/co.uk

Peter Beales offers a superb choice of over 1300 rose varieties, ranging from Shrub Roses and Bush Roses to Climbers, Ramblers and Ground-cover Roses, including 250 varieties that are unique to Peter Beales. There is also a lovely display garden.

Bill LeGrice Roses

Willow Farm, Cangate
Neatishead, Norfolk
NR12 8YH
Tel 01603 784466

www.rosebuddies.com

This family-run company has been in business for 90 years and has over 200 varieties for sale, including some unusually coloured roses, such as lilac, purple, brown and grey.

Cants of Colchester

Nayland Road, Mile End
Colchester, Essex
CO4 5EB
Tel 01206 844008
Fax 01206 855371

www.cantsroses.co.uk

Established in 1765, Cants is the oldest rose-grower in the country. Still family-run, they grow more than 70,000 roses, offered for sale by mail order each year.

C&K Jones

Golden Fields Nursery
Barrow Lane
Tarvin, Cheshire
CH3 8JF
Tel 01829 740663
Fax 01829 741877

C&K Jones grow over 70,000 roses for sale by mail order.

Cocker's Roses

Land Stracht, Aberdeen
AB15 6XH
Tel 01224 313261
Fax 01224 312531

www.roses.uk.com

A family-run business established in 1882, they are one of the foremost rose-breeders in the world.

Dickson Roses

42a Mile Cross Road
Newtownards, Co. Down
Northern Ireland
BT23 4SS
Tel 028 9181 2206
Fax 028 9181 3366

www.dickson-roses.co.uk

Founded in 1836, Dickson's principal business is rose breeding, but they have over 10,000 bare root roses for sale in the season.

Layham Garden Centre

Lower Road, Staple
Canterbury, Kent
CT3 1LH
01304 813267

Layham sells trees, shrubs, herbaceous plants, conifers, garden furniture and compost but specialises in roses.

Pococks

Jermyns Lane
Romsey, Hampshire
SO51 0QA
Tel/fax 10794 367500

www.pococksroses.co.uk

Pococks sells over 400 varieties of roses and produces 50,000 roses a year, which can also be viewed in their display field.

Rumwood Nurseries & Garden Centre

Langley
Maidstone, Kent
ME17 3ND
Tel 01622 861477
Fax 01622 863123

www.rumwoodnurseries.co.uk

With 35 years of experience in the industry, Rumwood Nurseries have over 400 varieties in their full catalogue, including their very own 'Maid of Kent'. There is also a Garden Centre selling trees, shrubs, hedging and bonsai as well as garden furniture. The catalogue is available online and in printed form.

And if you would like to track down some of the rarer French varieties:

Établissements Delbard

16 quai de la Mégisserie
75001 Paris
France
Tel (00 33) 820 310 345

www.delbard.com

Les roses anciennes

André Eve
ZA Morailles
45308 Pithiviers Cedex
Tel (00 33) 2 3830 0130

www.roses-anciennes-eve.com

Gardens to visit

City of Belfast International Rose Garden

Sir Thomas and
Lady Dixon Park
Upper Malone Road
Belfast
Northern Ireland

This award winning garden was begun in 1964 and boasts more than 30,000 rose bushes. It has four main features: Historical (traces the development of the garden rose), Heritage (breeds developed in Northern Ireland), Rose Trials (where new roses are trialled) and Display (where previous years' trials are left to grow on).

Elsing Hall Gardens

East Dereham
Norfolk
NR20 3DX
Tel 01362 637224
Open Sundays June–August

A beautiful moated, walled garden that specialises in Old Roses.

The Gardens of the Rose

Chiswell Green
St Albans, Herts
AL2 3NR
Tel 01727 850461
Fax 01727 850360
Email: mail@rnrs.org.uk
Open June–September

The flagship gardens of the Royal National Rose Society with over 30,000 rose varieties on display, complemented by a rich variety of companion plants, including 100 different clematis. Visit the Queen Mother Garden, which features displays of Old Roses, the International Trial Grounds, the Iris Garden and the Peace Rose Garden, among others.

Mannington Hall Gardens

Mannington Hall
Norwich
Norfolk
NR11 7BB
Tel 01263 584175

A 15th-century moated house surrounded by beautiful gardens featuring many different varieties of roses, from Ground-cover to Climbers. There is a Heritage Rose Garden and an area devoted to 20th-century roses.

Mottisfont Abbey Gardens

Mottisfont
Romsey, Hampshire
SO51 0LP
Tel 01794 340757/341220
(garden info)

www.nationaltrust.org.uk

Located by a tributary of the River Test and owned by the National Trust, Mottisfont is famous for its collection of Old Roses contained within its walled garden. There is interest all year round, but the display is at its best in mid-June.

Queen Mary's Rose Garden

Inner Circle
Regent's Park
London
NW1
Tel 020 7486 7905

London's largest and best rose garden with a good collection of many different rose varieties on display.

RHS Garden Rosemoor

Great Torrington
North Devon
EX38 8PH
Tel 01805 624067

www.rhs.org.uk

A Royal Horticultural Society garden which offers many different kinds of garden, including herb, cottage, herbaceous and kitchen gardens as well as a beautiful rose garden.

RHS Garden Wisley

Wisley
Woking, Surrey
GU23 6QB
Tel 01483 224234
Fax 01483 211750

www.rhs.org.uk

The principal and very extensive gardens of the Royal Horticultural Society, which feature many different rose varieties.

Royal Botanic Gardens

Kew
Richmond, Surrey
TW9 3AB
Tel 020 8332 5655
Fax 020 8332 5197

www.rbgkew.org.uk

Created in 1923, the rose garden at Kew has 54 rose beds, each containing a different variety. Ten beds illustrated the hybridisation of roses throughout the centuries.

Sissinghurst Castle Gardens

Sissinghurst
Nr Cranbrook, Kent
TN17 2AB
Tel 01580 710700/710701
(info line)

www.nationaltrust.org.uk

Owned by the National Trust and the former home of Vita Sackville-West and Sir Harold Nicolson, Sissinghurst is one of the most celebrated gardens in England.

St Anne's Rose Garden

St Anne's Park
Clontarf/Raheny
Dublin 3
Ireland
Tel (353) 1 83361859/8338898

In the grounds of the former home of the Guinness family (of brewery fame), every kind of rose is represented in this large rose garden, which was created in 1970.

Suggested further reading

The Old Rose Advisor
Brent C. Dickerson
Author's Choice Press

Growing Old-fashioned Roses
Trevor Nottle
Kangaroo Press

Growing Miniature & Patio Roses
Dawn and Barry Eagle
Cassell Illustrated

Old Roses and English Roses
David Austin
Antique Collector's Club

Reader's Digest Guide to Growing Roses
John Mattock
Reader's Digest

The Rose Gardens of England
Michael Gibson
Collins

Impressionist Roses
Friedman/Fairfax
Publishing

Designing with Roses
Tony Lord
Trafalgar Square

Author's acknowledgments and thanks

Had it not been for the garden with which I grew up, I would probably never have looked at the world – or at roses – in quite the same way. I have to thank my parents for having pushed open the metal gate of the old presbytery at Marnes-la-Coquette one summer's day in 1965.

Thanks to Jean-François for his ever-useful words of encouragement – and for his efforts with a spade, which are improving.

Thanks to Joëlle Caroline Mayer and Gilles Le Scanff, whose talents pay homage to the beauty of the rose.

Thanks to the whole team at Marabout, my French publishers, especially to Élisabeth, who gave me carte blanche, to Emmanuel Le Vallois, and to Rose-Marie, who had an ideal name!

Thanks to Edith Brochet-Lanvin for her meticulous reading. Our little disagreement on the famous question of the positioning below soil level of the grafting point proves, if proof were needed, that gardeners are all creatures with strong convictions and passionate opinions.

Thanks to roses for just 'being' – they always have the last word.

Joëlle Caroline Mayer and Gilles Le Scanff would like to thank all the gardeners in the following places, who helped them in various ways:

Château de la Bourlie at Urval (24) Dordogne
Domaine de St Jean de Beauregard at Les Ulis (91) Essonne
The Brochet-Lanvin Jardin botanique de la Presle at Nanteuil-la-Forêt (51) Marne
La Bonne Maison at Lyons (69) Rhône
La roseraie de Berty at Largentière (07) Ardèche
Le jardin d'Anne-Marie at Lardy (91) Essonne
Le jardin de Campagne at Grisy-les-Plâtres (95) Val d'Oise
Guy Thénot's garden
The garden at Talos (09) Ariège

The garden at Le Picou (09) Ariège
Les chemins de la rose at Doué la Fontaine (49) Maine-et-Loire
Les jardins de Bellevue at Beaumont le Hareng (76) Seine-Maritime
Les jardins du Prieuré Notre Dame d'Orsan at Maisonnais (18) Cher
Les roses anciennes André Eve at Morailles in Pithiviers-le-Vieil (45) Loiret
Meilland Richardier at Tassin La Demi Lune near Lyons (69) Rhône
Pépinières Delbard at Malicorne (03) Allier
Pépinière Maurice Laurent at St Romain-en-Gal (69) Rhône
La roseraie du Val-de-Marne at L'Haÿ-les-Roses (92) Val-de-Marne

Featured gardens:
Page 125 Le Maurissure; pages 127 and 129: Le Baqué; pages 129 and 141: Le jardin d'André Eve; page 131: Le jardin de campagne; page 133 Le Potager de l'Émière; page 137: Le jardin de l'Alchimiste.

All the photographs that appear in this book were taken by Joëlle Caroline Mayer and Gilles Le Scanff, except for the following:
• Eléonor Cruse, Roseraie de Berty: *Rosa arvensis* 'Splendens' (page 117)
• Agence Map, Arnaud Descat: *Rosa* 'William Lobb' (page 52), 'Magic Meillandecor' (page 90), *Rosa* 'Crimson Glory' (page 70), *Rosa* 'Grand Mère Jenny' (page 71), *Rosa* 'Erfurt' (page 44).
• Agence Map, Frédéric Didillon: *Rosa spinosissima* 'Altaica' (page 80)
• Agence Map, N and P Mioulane: *Rosa* 'Thérèse Bugnet (page 120)

The diagrams on pages 34-35 were created by the WAG studio.

The publisher would like to thank:
• Edith Brochet-Lanvin, rose specialist at the Jardin Botanique de la Presle, for her careful checking.
• Nathalie Becq, rose-specialist at Jardin à la Campagne, for permitting us to take photographs among her roses.
• Patrick Bouchard from the Roseraie du Val-de-Marne at L'Haÿ-les-Roses for his collaboration on the choice of photographs.